NEW ESSAYS ON NATIVE SON

★ The American Novel ★

GENERAL EDITOR

Emory Elliott
University of California, Riverside

Other books in the series:
New Essays on The Scarlet Letter
New Essays on The Great Gatsby
New Essays on Adventures of Huckleberry Finn
New Essays on Moby-Dick
New Essays on Uncle Tom's Cabin
New Essays on The Red Badge of Courage
New Essays on The Sun Also Rises
New Essays on The American
New Essays on Light in August
New Essays on Invisible Man
New Essays on The Awakening
New Essays on The Portrait of a Lady

New Essays on
Native Son

Edited by
Keneth Kinnamon

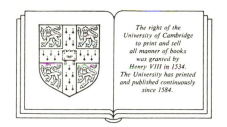

*The right of the
University of Cambridge
to print and sell
all manner of books
was granted by
Henry VIII in 1534.
The University has printed
and published continuously
since 1584.*

CAMBRIDGE UNIVERSITY PRESS

Cambridge

New York   Port Chester   Melbourne   Sydney

Published by the Press Syndicate of the University of Cambridge
The Pitt Building, Trumpington Street, Cambridge CB2 1RP
40 West 20th Street, New York, NY 10011, USA
10 Stamford Road, Oakleigh, Melbourne 3166, Australia

A similar version of the essay by Houston A. Baker, Jr. first appeared in
The Workings of the Spirit: The Poetics of Black Women's Writing published by
The University of Chicago Press, 1990

First published 1990

Printed in the United States of America

Library of Congress Cataloging-in-Publication Data

New essays on Native son : edited by Keneth Kinnamon.
p.   cm. – (The American novel)
Includes bibliographical references.
ISBN 0-521-34319-4
1. Wright, Richard, 1908–1960. Native son.   2. Afro-Americans in literature.
I. Wright, Richard, 1908–1960. Native son.
II. Kinnamon, Keneth. II. Series.
PS3545.R815N343   1990
813'.52 – dc20   89-28001

British Library Cataloging in Publication data applied for.

ISBN 0-521-34319-4 hardback
ISBN 0-521-34822-6 paperback

Contents

v

Contents

vi

Series Editor's Preface

In literary criticism the last twenty-five years have been particularly fruitful. Since the rise of the New Criticism of the 1950s, which focused attention of critics and readers upon the text itself – apart from history, biography, and society – there has emerged a wide variety of critical methods which have brought to literary works a rich diversity of perspectives: social, historical, political, psychological, economic, ideological, and philosophical. While attention to the text itself, as taught by the New Critics, remains at the core of contemporary interpretation, the widely shared assumption that works of art generate many different kinds of interpretation has opened up possibilities for new readings and new meanings.

Before this critical revolution, many American novels had come to be taken for granted by earlier generations of readers as having an established set of recognized interpretations. There was a sense among many students that the canon was established and that the larger thematic and interpretive issues had been decided. The task of the new reader was to examine the ways in which elements such as structure, style, and imagery contributed to each novel's acknowledged purpose. But recent criticism has brought these old assumptions into question and has thereby generated a wide variety of original, and often quite surprising, interpretations of the classics, as well as of rediscovered novels such as Kate Chopin's *The Awakening*, which has only recently entered the canon of works that scholars and critics study and that teachers assign their students.

The aim of The American Novel Series is to provide students of American literature and culture with introductory critical guides to

American novels now widely read and studied. Each volume is devoted to a single novel and begins with an introduction by the volume editor, a distinguished authority on the text. The introduction presents details of the novel's composition, publication history, and contemporary reception, as well as a survey of the major critical trends and readings from first publication to the present. This overview is followed by four or five original essays, specifically commissioned from senior scholars of established reputation and from outstanding younger critics. Each essay presents a distinct point of view, and together they constitute a forum of interpretative methods and of the best contemporary ideas on each text.

It is our hope that these volumes will convey the vitality of current critical work in American literature, generate new insights and excitement for students of the American novel, and inspire new respect for and new perspectives upon these major literary texts.

Emory Elliott
University of California, Riverside

1

Introduction

KENETH KINNAMON

1

LIKE Henry James and Thomas Wolfe, Richard Wright is his own best critic, at least on matters pertaining to the conception and composition of his greatest novel. In person and on paper he was ready to explain the genesis of *Native Son* (1940), analyze its personal and political significance, and defend it from racist attack. As a militant black Communist writer, winner of the *Story* magazine contest for employees of the Federal Writers Project for *Uncle Tom's Children* (1938) as well as second prize in the *O. Henry Memorial Award Prize Stories of 1938* for "Fire and Cloud," he was already an experienced lecturer as he was completing his novel in the late winter and spring of 1939. In February of that year he lectured at the Harlem Community Center on "Negro Culture in New York"; in May he spoke at the Brooklyn YMCA on "The Cultural Contributions of the Negro in America"; and in September he appeared with Langston Hughes and the Communist politician James W. Ford at the Festival of Negro Culture in Chicago. He may not have discussed his forthcoming work on these occasions, but he probably did so back in New York in a guest appearance in his friend Edwin Seaver's writing class at the New School for Social Research on December 8, 1939; in a lecture on "The Problems of the Fiction Writer Today" at the Dalcroze School of Music on January 26, 1940, under the auspices of the League of American Writers; and in a talk the following month in Chicago at the Woodlawn A.M.E. Church.[1]

I am grateful to Ellen Wright for granting me permission to use and quote from restricted material in her late husband's papers at Yale. Without her generous cooperation this introduction would not have been possible.

Native Son was published on March 1, 1940, to great critical acclaim. Within two weeks Wright had spoken at Columbia University and at the 135th Street Branch of the New York Public Library on "How 'Bigger' Was Born," a lecture he repeated in July at the Church of the Good Shepherd in Chicago and at the White Rock Baptist Church in Durham, North Carolina, and in September at a gala fund-raiser for the Negro Playwrights Company at the Golden Gate Ballroom in Harlem.[2] A condensed version appeared in print in the *Saturday Review* in June, followed by a more drastic condensation in the September–October issue of *Negro Digest*. Sales figures on *Native Son* were excellent in March and April, but when they began to fade in May, Wright's editor at Harper's, Edward Aswell, proposed a "documentary edition" (later called "author's edition") of the novel with an appendix containing the full text of "How 'Bigger' Was Born," David L. Cohn's hostile review of *Native Son* in the May issue of *The Atlantic Monthly,* and Wright's rebuttal of Cohn.[3] When Cohn understandably refused to go along with this scheme, Harper's published the complete *How "Bigger" Was Born* as a pamphlet. Grosset & Dunlap included the pamphlet version as a preface to its inexpensive reprint of *Native Son* in 1942, and it has been reprinted several times since.

In *How "Bigger" Was Born* Wright recalls and analyzes the long gestation of *Native Son* in the experiences of his childhood in the South. Restless and rebellious, the Bigger type Wright observed (and to a degree himself embodied) both defied the racist order and withdrew from the black culture which provided nurture and compensation to those who could accommodate their lives to the system of white supremacy. The first example Wright cites appears to be merely a schoolyard bully, but as other examples unfold, his violent, aggressive personality comes to seem generic, his sadism his only means of self-realization. The other four southern Biggers described by Wright turned from brutalizing other blacks to direct confrontation with the white world. Bigger No. 2 declined to pay his rent or his debts for food and clothing, refusing to recognize the legitimacy of the racist economic system which denied an adequate supply of these essentials to black people. The third Bigger moved a step further by taking his recreation without paying the white man for it, habitually walking into a motion picture theater without a ticket. Bigger No. 4, a more intellectual type with a manic-depressive personality, violated racial taboos of all kinds, refused to work, brooded and joked about racial injustice, and ended up in an insane asylum. The fifth Bigger specialized in boarding streetcars without paying and sitting in the white section, defying with knife in hand the white conductor's orders to move. These exhilarating gestures of rebellion were necessarily of brief duration in a Jim Crow society: "Eventually, the whites who restricted their lives made them pay a terrible price. They were shot, hanged, maimed, lynched, and generally hounded until they were either dead or their spirits broken."[4]

For historical reasons, Wright explains, black reaction to the conditions of southern life tended toward the extremes of rebellion and submission, the latter category including both drunks and strivers, Uncle Toms and blues men. The rebellious Bigger type, though, was both estranged from the folk culture and attracted to the promise and glamour of the white life to which he was denied access. First understanding the Bigger phenomenon only in these racial terms, Wright added the dimension of class to caste through his contact with Communism, somewhat euphemistically called in *How "Bigger" Was Born* "the labor movement and its ideology." Bigger could be white as well as black, and his rebellious personality held a revolutionary potential that could seek either Communist or fascist fulfillment. Although Wright had already encountered problems with party functionaries and was to denounce his former comrades bitterly in *The Outsider* (1953), he could hardly have been more emphatic in declaring the importance of that deepened understanding of the Bigger type made possible by Marxist thought: "The extension of my sense of the personality of Bigger was the pivot of my life; it altered the complexion of my existence. . . . It was as though I had put on a pair of spectacles whose power was that of an x-ray enabling me to see deeper into the lives of men."[5] Critics who read *Native Son* as a black nationalist repudiation of Marxism — Bigger's instinctive black triumph over Boris Max's arid white theorizing — would do well to ponder these words. Wright's effort in the novel is to reconcile his sense of black life with the intellectual clarity and the possibility of social action provided by Communism, to interpret each group to the other. What he would soon be writing to explain his revolutionary verse of the mid-thirties applies equally well to *Native Son*, though his audience for the novel was much larger: "I would address my words to two groups: I would tell Communists how common people felt, and I would tell common people of the self-sacrifice of Communists who strove for unity among them."[6]

Further exposure to the urban Biggers of Chicago, more explosive even than the Biggers of the South, deepened Wright's understanding of the type, as did his further reading in white literature reflecting the frenetic life of cities and his close study of Biggers in pre-Revolutionary Russia and in Nazi Germany. "Tense, afraid, nervous, hysterical, and restless," Wright explains, the Bigger Thomas of his novel is the "product of a dislocated society; he is a dispossessed and disinherited man; he is all of this, and he lives amid the greatest possible plenty on earth and he is looking and feeling for a way out." Obstacles to telling the truth about such a character were formidable, but Bigger had so captivated Wright's imagination that he resolved to portray him, determined to do justice to all the dimensions of his complex character and significance: his individual consciousness in all its subjectivity; his ambivalent feelings as a black native son toward the country that excludes him; the existential qualities of "primal fear and dread"[7] that are the psychological basis of all our lives, underlying and conditioning our social experience; the political meaning of Bigger's life; his relationship with other blacks; his raw Chicago environment.

In *How "Bigger" Was Born* Wright states that his exposure to urban Biggers while working at the South Side Boys' Club coalesced the years of brooding about the type and prompted him to begin the actual writing of the novel. The year was 1935. Probably he only sketched preliminary notes, for at this time he was busy writing poetry and the posthumously published *Lawd Today* (1963). More sustained work began in New York early in 1938. The first reviews of *Uncle Tom's Children* persuaded him that an even more unflinching confrontation with the full dimensions of racism was necessary: "I found that I had written a book which even bankers' daughters could read and feel good about. I swore to myself that if I ever wrote another book, no one would weep over it; that it would be so hard and deep that they would have to face it without the consolation of tears. It was this that made me get to work in dead earnest."[8] Moving to Brooklyn on April 13 to live with Chicago friends Jane and Herbert Newton, Wright worked intensely on his novel through the spring, summer, and early fall, completing a first draft of 576 pages by October 24.[9]

The rebellious young black men Wright had himself observed in the South and the North became collectively the prototype of his protagonist, but as if to validate the literary character another Bigger, whom Wright never saw, emerged from obscurity late in May and affected the novel even more directly than his earlier counterparts. As Wright was nearing the midway point of his first draft, two young black men, Robert Nixon and Earl Hicks, were arrested in Chicago and charged with the murder of a white woman. Nixon became the central figure in the case, which received sensationalized coverage in the Chicago press, especially the openly racist *Tribune*. One article, for example, asserted that "civilization has left Nixon practically untouched. His hunched shoulders and long, sinewy arms that dangle almost to his knees; his out-thrust head and catlike tread all suggest the animal. . . . He is very black – almost pure Negro. His physical characteristics suggest an earlier link in the species." The reporter continued: "A jungle negro, this type is known to be ferocious and relentless in a fight. Though docile enough under ordinary circumstances, they are easily aroused. And when this happens the veneer of civilization disappears." And as if the simian imagery were not already obvious enough, Nixon is said to kill "with a ferocity suggestive of Poe's 'Murders in the Rue Morgue' – the work of a giant ape."[10] As soon as Wright heard about this case, early in June, he wrote his friend Margaret Walker in Chicago, asking her for newspaper clippings on the Nixon case. Walker complied, collecting all the clippings from all the Chicago dailies. So assiduous was she that "he had enough to spread all over his nine by twelve bedroom floor and he was using them in the same way Dreiser had done in *American Tragedy*. He would spread them all out and read them over and over again and then take off from there in his own imagination."[11]

Not content with press coverage of the Nixon case, Wright traveled to Chicago in November to gather additional information. A typed agenda for this trip shows how thorough and meticulous Wright was in accumulating naturalistic details to assure the verisimilitude of his Chicago setting.[12] The Nixon case both stimulated his imagination and provided him material, but he shaped the material to his thematic purpose. Newspaper coverage of Bigger Thomas, the inquest, and the trial corresponds in many details to that of the Nixon case, but elsewhere Wright makes significant changes to develop his ideological points. Nixon's first attorney was Joseph Roth of the International Labor Defense, but he was soon replaced by black lawyers of the National Negro Congress, who represented Nixon at the trial. By eliminating black legal representation and magnifying the role of the white radical Boris Max, Wright accomplishes two purposes. As a Communist, Max can articulate a Marxist analysis of Bigger's situation that clearly derives from Wright's own conceptual analysis of the effects of racism on the Bigger type.[13] At the same time, in the final scene Wright can contrast Bigger's black emotional apprehension of the meaning of his ordeal with Max's white intellectual interpretation of it, a contrast of complementary understandings not possible if Wright had followed the Nixon case and provided Bigger with black lawyers. Another change also shows Wright's Communist perspective in *Native Son*. After Nixon was arrested for the murder of Mrs. Florence Johnson, Chicago police used third-degree methods to extract from him confessions, later withdrawn, of other crimes, including the murder of another woman a year earlier, when he was alleged to have written the words "Black Legion" with his victim's lipstick on her bedroom mirror. The Black Legion, as Humphrey Bogart fans will recall from a film about the group, was an extremist right-wing organization in Detroit and other midwestern cities, a kind of northern urban version of the Ku Klux Klan. When Bigger thinks of diverting suspicion from himself, he signs the ransom note "Red" and draws a hammer and sickle. By changing from fascists to Communists, Wright implies that the latter share with Bigger the role of social outcast, a point Max emphasizes later in the novel.[14]

Most of *How "Bigger" Was Born* is devoted to Bigger himself, but at the end of the essay Wright turns to the actual process of writing the novel, concentrating on the tension between truth and plausibility, the varieties of narrative technique used while maintaining and projecting Bigger's perspective, the opening and closing scenes written after the first draft, and, briefly, the process of revision. This remarkable exercise in literary autoanalysis concludes by placing *Native Son* and its subject in the context of the American tradition in fiction: "We do have in the Negro the embodiment of a past tragic enough to appease the spiritual hunger of even a James; and we have in the oppression of the Negro a shadow athwart our national life dense and heavy enough to satisfy even the gloomy broodings of a Hawthorne. And if Poe were alive, he would not have to invent horror; horror would invent him."[15]

2

As revealing as *How "Bigger" Was Born* is, it does not tell us everything about the composition of *Native Son*. An examination of letters, notes, manuscripts, and galley and page proofs at Yale, Princeton, the Schomburg Collection, and the Fales Collection of New York University supplements the essay in rewarding ways. These materials show in detail Wright's evolving conception of his novel and the artistry with which he articulated, shaped, and refined it. They also show how others seem to have participated in this creative process, notably his literary agent Paul Reynolds, his editor Edward Aswell, and the author of the introduction, Dorothy Canfield Fisher. My somewhat cursory examination of these materials allows me to make some preliminary observations and reach some tentative conclusions, but they await and require more thorough and detailed investigation.

After completing his first draft, Wright began to revise his book, a process that continued for over a year.[16] Large and small changes were made, most on Wright's own initiative but some suggested by others. Stylistic revision usually moved toward clarity, more precise diction, or greater economy of expression. For example, the Schomburg version's "another cigarette in his lips" becomes the more vivid "another cigarette slanting across his chin" in the published novel. The prolix "Bigger took a deep breath and looked from face to face, as though it seemed to him the height [sic] of foolishness that he should have to explain" is compressed to "Bigger took a deep breath and looked from face to face. It seemed to him that he should not have to explain" (pp. 11, 21 [16, 27]).[17] The word *ofays,* unintelligible to most white readers, is changed to *white folks* in the novel as published.[18] In addition to authorial revisions on almost every page of the Schomburg typescript of the first draft, several inserts in Wright's hand make more extensive changes.

As the manuscript evolved, Wright altered his representation of dialogue in various ways. The phrase "said Bigger" and similar locutions are changed to "Bigger said."[19] The intermediate version's representation of Jan and Mary's drunken speech ("Gosh-bye, shoney" and "shome") is softened in the novel ("Goo'bye, honey" and "some") to avoid an inappropriate comic quality shortly before Mary is killed. Wright's rendering of black dialect in *Native Son* contrasts in a significant way to his earlier practice. In an early draft of his short story "Down by the Riverside," probably completed in 1935, he writes dialect as dialect whether using a typewriter or a pencil: "Naw, Lawd. Ah cant break down like this . . . Theyll know somethings wrong if Ah ack like this" or "Ah wan some watah."[20] In *Native Son* Wright's usual method is to write standard English speech and then change the spelling to produce dialect, as in these two examples from the speech of Reverend Hammond:[21]

```
     aw            Y
Lord Jesus, turn your eyes and look with mercy upon us sinners.
l        er                          Yuh
Look into the heart of this poor lost boy. You said that mercy
uz
was always Yours.


    e   i
Forget everything but your fate son.
```

In his broad dialect as well as his submissive Christianity, Reverend Hammond is an anachronistic remnant of a black southern culture rapidly being changed by the altered conditions of northern urban life. None of the other black characters, not even Mrs. Thomas, speaks as he does. Wright's new method of creating such dialect surely results from his own estrangement from his southern past.

On a much larger scale, Wright made important changes that greatly improved the opening and closing episodes of the novel. In the original version of the opening scene, Bigger is not awakened by the clanging alarm clock which also awakens the reader to the squalid realities of life in a black slum, but by knocking on the door of the Thomas family's kitchenette apartment in Chicago. The caller is Sister Mosley, a church friend of Mrs. Thomas, who has dropped by on her way to work to leave tickets to be sold for an Easter rally. The long and tedious dialogue between Bigger, his mother, and Sister Mosley occupies most of sixteen typed pages. Bigger's street friend Jack arrives shortly after the departure of Sister Mosley, but Mrs. Thomas refuses to let him in. Filled with disgust by Sister Mosley's importunate solicitude for the state of his soul and his mother's incessant scolding and nagging, Bigger clearly prefers the secular street to the sacred storefront. Deriving from Wright's own rejection of religion as the opiate of the black people, the scene does prepare the way for Bigger's later rejection of Reverend Hammond (here first called Temple), but the scene lacks any drama except verbal bickering and fails to emphasize the squalor of the South Side environment.[22] In *How "Bigger" Was Born* Wright explains that one night while drinking he thought of a battle with a rat: "At first I rejected the idea . . . I was afraid that the rat would 'hog' the scene. But the rat would not leave me . . . So, cautioning myself to allow the rat scene to disclose *only* Bigger, his family, their little room, and their relationships, I let the rat walk in, and he did his stuff."[23] The rat's stuff was powerful stuff indeed, creating some of the most effective opening pages in American fiction. Economically and above all dramatically, the scene deftly establishes the relationship between all four members of the Thomas household (not just between Bigger and his mother), exposes the sordid and crowded conditions of their existence, shows the incipient violence of Bigger's personality, and, additionally, symbolically foreshadows Bigger's fate as a black "rat" hunted down by a remorseless and powerful foe. The importance of the change can hardly be overestimated. The excitement of the rat scene rivets the reader's attention to a tense narrative. If the novel had been published with the omitted original opening, many bored readers would have put the book down after the first few pages.

The original conclusion to *Native Son* was also changed, but by deletion rather than substitution. Wright's explanation in *How "Bigger" Was Born* is incomplete: "In the first draft I had Bigger going smack to the electric chair; but I felt that two murders were enough for one novel. I cut the final scene . . ."[24] The problem, however, seems not so much another violent death as overwriting for a self-conscious poetic effect. In Wright's developmental notes for the novel is a typed sheet headed "POETIC MOTIFS TO BE WOVEN INTO FINAL SCENE," consisting of seven items, the last of which reads "Most important of all poetic motifs is that of life being a deep. [sic] exciting and entralling [sic] adventure; that is the note on which the book should end to carry over the promise and feeling of something which must happen in the future I MUST SPEAK IN POETIC TERMS OF THIS."[25] To do so he drew upon a central metaphor of his creative imagination – fire. Fire figures prominently in such early poems as "Between the World and Me," "Everywhere Burning Waters Rise," and "Obsession," as well as in three of the four stories of *Uncle Tom's Children*. In the final story of that collection, "Fire and Cloud," the protagonist tells his followers: "Ah *know* now! Ah done seen the *sign!* Wes gotta git together. Ah know whut yo life is! Ah done felt it! It's *fire!*"[26] *Black Boy* begins its narrative of Wright's early life with the episode of his setting fire to his house at the age of four. The central event in the plot of *The Long Dream* is a terrible fire in a black night club based on the actual holocaust of the Rhythm Nite Club in Natchez, Mississippi, in 1940.[27]

Unlike most of these instances, however, the metaphorical dimension of fire in the original conclusion of *Native Son* does not proceed from an actual conflagration, but exists only in a vague and implausible dream world of Bigger's imagination: "The picture enclosed him about, shutting the world out from him, making it a dream of restless shadows, and giving him a sense of being near an invisible but glowing center of fire, at the border of a land filled with a strange stillness." As the time for execution arrives, a guard comes

10

to his cell and orders him to *"sit up kid."* Bigger struggles to maintain the purity of his vision by rejecting this demand of the actual world: "The voice came to him from faraway, and instead of calling him from his vision of many men who were sparks and all men who were a flame of life, instead of making him recede from the boundaries of that silent land where his senses felt a new and strange peace, the voice drew him closer. The heat of that flame, invisible but strong with its heat, and the silence and stillness of that land were so deep he could heat [sic] it." As the legs of his pants are being slit for placement of the electrodes, he thinks: "A short time and then he would be englufed [sic] in that ever widening yellow flame of fire leaping from a ball of fire. A short time and then he would walk into that new and strange land, with its still silence." In the brief space of the final page and a half of the first draft, the "fiercely glowing flame of fire and the silence of that new and still land" recur seven times, culminating in the moment of death in the electric chair: "In a split second he knew that death was near and the flame became a huge fiery sun suspended just above him, in front of his eyes, and his arms were open to embrace it and walk into that land beyond the sun and then he sprang forward to it, his dry lips kissing the hot fire; he felt a dark silent explosion and he was in the blinding light of a new and unseen day, enwrapped in the silence of a land beyond the sun." Thus metaphor becomes metonymy. How much more effective the ending became when Wright cut this repetitious and overblown rhetoric, chastened his propensity for poeticizing, and avoided the sensationalism of an attempt to render the moment of electrocution. Having affirmed the terrible knowledge of his self-realization through murder; having parted from Max, who understands him well as social symbol but only imperfectly as human being; and having won through to a sense of equality by calling Jan simply by his first name rather than referring to him as Mister Jan, thus speaking to a white as whites speak to blacks – having accomplished these things Bigger is left in existential solitude as the simple, monosyllabic concluding sentences sound the knell of that fate which inexorably follows his fear and flight: "He still held on to the bars. Then he smiled a faint, wry, bitter smile. He heard the ring of steel against steel as a far door clanged shut" (p. 359 [392]).

11

Suggestions about revising the opening and closing scenes may have been made by such friends as Jane Newton, Theodore Ward, and Ralph Ellison, but the changes, essentially Wright's, were in place by the time he showed the novel to his agent Paul Reynolds in February 1939. In a letter on the last day of that month Reynolds wrote that he found the first part "very impressive" but wished that "it had a little more humor." After completing his reading of the entire manuscript, he reported to Wright early in March with praise of Bigger, the other black characters, and Max. He found the other white characters implausible, however, and also suggested cutting the "Fate" section, especially the courtroom scenes and the newspaper material. Six weeks later Reynolds wrote that Edward Aswell, the editor at Harper's, "has nearly finished your novel and he asks if you could come in to see him next Tuesday. . . . I think he has in mind certain revision, if you agree." By May 11 Reynolds was wishing "all power . . . with the revision," and on June 16 he reported that Aswell "is very keen about the book and thinks you did a swell job of the revision. He said there were two or three minor points he would like to discuss with you."[28]

Wright followed the suggestion of his agent to cut the last section of the novel, but we do not know exactly what revisions were agreed to in conference with Aswell. Nevertheless, it seems likely that their discussion focused on the controversial subjects of sex and politics, for much of the later revision of the manuscript consisted of deletion of passages concerning these matters.

An attentive reader must pause in Book Three over a point State's Attorney Buckley makes while grilling Bigger. Attempting to implicate him in various unsolved crimes and to break him down for confession, Buckley mentions the planned robbery of Blum's delicatessen and then goes on: "You didn't think I knew about that, did you? I know a lot more, boy. I know about that dirty trick you and your friend Jack pulled off in the Regal Theatre, too. You wonder how I know it? The manager told us when we were checking up. I know what boys like you do, Bigger" (p. 260 [284]). What dirty trick? The reader going back to Book One finds none. The solution to this puzzle is that the quoted passage, which Wright neglected to delete for consistency, refers to an episode of masturbation by Bigger and Jack in the darkened theater that went through the various drafts all the way to galley proof before being crossed out. Bigger and Jack are hardly seated when the graphic description begins: "'I'm polishing my nightstick,' Bigger said."[29] Seen by a passing woman, Bigger and Jack are reported to the manager.[30] The masturbation scene continues for a full page, ending when the two change seats because of the mess they have made.

As the original version of the episode in the Regal Theatre continues, the movie begins with a newsreel showing wealthy young white women on a Florida beach. One of these is Mary Dalton, who is shown in a close-up embracing Jan Erlone as the narrator comments: *"Mary Dalton, daughter of Chicago's Henry Dalton, 4605 Drexel Boulevard, shocks society by spurning the boys of La Salle Street and the Gold Coast and accepting the attentions of a well-known radical while on her recent winter vacation in Florida."* Other sexy scenes with mildly lewd comments by the narrator follow. Recognizing the address as the one at which he will make application for employment that very afternoon, Bigger and Jack discuss the sexual possibilities with Mary. With this deleted passage in mind, it is easy to understand Bigger's otherwise implausible speculation in the novel as published: "Maybe he [Mr. Dalton] had a daughter who was a hot kind of girl" (p. 29 [36]).

Before the changes in galley proof, then, Wright was presenting Bigger as a typically highly sexed nineteen-year-old who had been titillated by a newsreel showing the scantily clad Mary kissing and embracing her lover. He is soon to witness such scenes in person, for that night he chauffeurs Mary and Jan, who make love in the back seat while Bigger drives them around Washington Park: "He looked at the mirror. Mary was lying flat on her back in the rear seat and Jan was bent over her. He saw a faint sweep of white thigh. They plastered all right, he thought. He pulled the car softly round the curves, looking at the road before him one second and up at the mirror the next. He heard Jan whispering; then he heard them both sigh. Filled with a sense of them, his muscles grew gradually taut. He sighed and sat up straight, fighting off the stiffening feeling in his loins. But soon he was slouched again. His lips were numb. I'm almost drunk, he thought. His sense of the city and park fell away; he was floating in the car and Jan and Mary were in back kissing, spooning. A long time passed. Jan sat up and pulled Mary with him." After expurgations in galley proof, the passage as published deletes all mention of Bigger's arousal: "He looked at the mirror; they were drinking again. They plastered, all right, he thought. He pulled the car softly round the curves, looking at the road before him one second and up at the mirror the next. He heard Jan whispering; then he heard them both sigh. His lips were numb. I'm almost drunk, he thought. His sense of the city and park fell away; he was floating in the car and Jan and Mary were in back, kissing. A long time passed" (pp. 67–8 [78]).

Similar deletions are made in the following scene in the Dalton house, when Bigger carries the drunken Mary to her room and puts her to bed. In the published version Bigger kisses Mary and "she swayed against him" (p. 73 [84]), but the deleted galley passage continues more explicitly: "He tightened his arms as his lips pressed tightly against hers and he felt her body moving strongly. The thought and conviction that Jan had had her a lot flashed through his mind. He kissed her again and felt the sharp bones of her hips move in a hard and veritable grind. Her mouth was open and her breath came slow and deep." A marginal note beside the passage in an editor's hand, probably Aswell's,[31] reads "suggest cutting this." Later, as Bigger is having sex with his girlfriend Bessie Mears, he fantasizes that she is Mary. This scene was retained in the galleys and changed only in page proof.

Because explicit interracial sexual scenes had never appeared in serious American fiction, Wright's conception of Bigger as a highly sexed, poor young black man with a physical interest in a wild, rich young white woman was daring indeed. Bankers' daughters reading such a story would be titillated or shocked, but they would certainly not be moved to tears of compassion for Bigger. As Aswell knew, and as he must have argued to Wright, to retain such highly charged sexual scenes would risk censorship and thus prevent the larger political message from being conveyed, or at best undercut that message by diverting the salacious reader's attention. For whatever reason, the changes were made, resulting in a softened, less threatening, more victimized Bigger, one over whom bankers' daughters might weep after all.

The other significant category of changes from manuscript and proof to published novel is political. Here it is more difficult to separate Wright's artistic imperatives from thematic changes suggested by others. Many readers of *Native Son* have been bothered by the prolixity of Book Three, especially the long speeches of both attorneys. Wright himself was quite aware of the problem, for his developmental notes contain such self-admonitions as the following: "How much of Max's examination of Bigger can be transferred to early pages. . . . Compress Buckley's speech. . . . Cut or compress newspaper articles where they can be don [sic] so."[32] Buckley's speech was compressed by a half-page, but more extensive cuts were made in Boris Max's plea to the court. The published version (pp. 324–39 [353–70]), which, as Dr. Johnson said of *Paradise Lost*, none ever wished longer than it is, was in fact five pages longer in galley proof. It would be difficult to argue that the longer version is more effective, but some interesting material was cut. Early in the galley version Max emphasizes the public hysteria accompanying Bigger's trial: "the low, angry muttering of that mob which the state troops are holding back . . . the hungry yelping of hounds on the hunt." The implicit comparison of Bigger to a fugitive slave adds historical resonance, but Wright must have realized – or Aswell may have reminded him – that the threat of a lynch mob storming a courthouse was not plausible in the city of Chicago, however many times it had happened in the South. Other cuts involved such topics as anti-Semitism, naive white liberalism, the social barriers between Bigger and Mary, and the analogy – a familiar one in Afro-American literature – between black rebelliousness and the American Revolution. Cumulatively these deletions have the effect of toning down slightly the political message of Book Three, though they also mitigate the artistic tedium their inclusion would increase.

Other cuts in Max's speech are necessary for consistency. Having dropped the original ending of the novel, Wright omits from the galleys passages about "life, new and strange" and passages invoking fire imagery: "Bigger Thomas is part of a furious blaze of liquid life energy which once blazed and is still blazing in our land. He is a hot jet of life that spattered itself in futility against a cold wall." Here Wright may have been uneasy with the orgasmic hyperbole of such a metaphor. Certainly other cuts de-emphasized Bigger's sexuality, such as the deletion of a reference to masturbation as a trope for Bigger's entire life. In Buckley's speech, too, Wright cuts a reference to the Florida newsreel and "the obnoxious sexual perversions practiced by these boys in darkened theatres."

Still other deletions may have occurred to Wright independently or have been suggested by Aswell or others. At one point Max is considering the paradoxes of racism. A white chauffeur arriving with the drunken daughter of his employer, he argues, would have informed him of her condition, but racist treatment of Bigger "made him do the *very* thing we did not want." Max goes farther: "Or, am I wrong? Maybe we *wanted* him to do it! Maybe we would have had no chance or justification to stage attacks against hundreds of thousands of people if he had acted sanely and normally! Maybe we would have had to go to the expensive length of inventing theories to justify our attacks if we had treated him fairly!" Such implausible and involuted speculation justifies deletion, but the cumulative effect of cuts involving racial politics, like that of those concerning Bigger's sexuality, is to lower the stridency of Wright's message, to soften the characterization, perhaps even to dilute the theme. One can maintain plausibly that deletions enhanced the literary value of Book Three, or even that more cuts would have improved it further, but the fact remains that Wright finally decided or was persuaded to let Max say less than he had said through the drafts and unrevised galleys. In the case of *Native Son*, Edward Aswell, a white liberal from Tennessee and Harvard who had been Thomas Wolfe's editor and was to become Wright's valued friend, may even be regarded as standing in relation to Wright as Max stands in relation to Bigger: sympathetic, loyal, analytical, understanding to a point, but not quite ready to accept the full and uncut expression of a sensibility so radically different from his own.

Moreover, Aswell decided at the last minute not to let *Native Son* go unmediated into the world. In the early summer of 1939 the Book-of-the-Month Club had expressed interest in the novel. On September 23 his literary agent wrote Wright optimistically: "We have always understood that Dorothy Canfield has as much or more influence in the Book-of-the-Month Club than anyone else so I am really quite hopeful though I don't know anything about it." Fisher, a productive and well-known writer, was a member of the board of selection. The matter dragged on for the rest of the year, delaying publication by several months. Never before had the Book-of-the-Month Club selected a novel by a black writer. Finally, early in the new year, Aswell wrote with the good news that the book had been selected as a March alternate. Furthermore, he noted that "Dorothy Canfield Fisher has written a brief Introduction." Nine days later he expressed satisfaction with Fisher's effort and his regret that Wright had not had an opportunity to see it: "Under ordinary circumstances, if there had been more time, we should have wanted to consult you before deciding to put in it [sic]. Pressed as we were, I took the responsibility of saying that I felt pretty sure you would approve. I hope I have not guessed wrong." Presented with a fait accompli and the likelihood that the Book-of-the-Month Club would not accept the novel as a selection without the introduction, Wright could do little but assent with as much grace as he could muster. After another week Aswell wrote: "I am glad you liked Dorothy Canfield's Introduction."[33]

What we have here is a latter-day example of the process of white authentication which Robert Stepto has shown to be so characteristic a feature of slave narratives.[34] In that process a well-known white abolitionist would provide a preface, guarantee, or letter attesting to the veracity or historicity of the narrative and the genuineness of the author's credentials. Only with such a seal of approval, the feeling was, would a predominantly white audience be receptive to a black story. The difficulty was that the authenticator's white perspective inevitably distorted as it mediated the necessarily different black perspective of the author. So we have Max and Bigger again – or Aswell and Wright.

Dorothy Canfield Fisher of Arlington, Vermont, was an influential and energetic white liberal who had produced a steady stream of books since the first decade of the century. Nevertheless, her credentials as a commentator on black life and letters were minimal: membership on the board of trustees of Howard University and treatment of a light family passing for white in the subplot of an early novel (*The Bent Twig*, 1915). Her most recent novel, *Seasoned Timber* (1939), had been an attack on anti-Semitism. It must have seemed to Aswell that her heart was in the right place, and there could be little doubt that her endorsement would help sales. Her brief introduction is accurately characterized by Robert Stepto as "innocently vapid,"[35] but it is also confused, offering two opposed interpretations of Bigger. First, he is compared to a laboratory rat or sheep frustrated by the denial of fulfillment in American society. Then, as if to compensate for this emphasis on environmental determinism, she describes the theme of *Native Son* as "the Dostoievski subject — a human soul in hell because it is sick with a deadly spiritual sickness" (p. x). She raises two points which many reviewers and readers seized upon, but she makes no effort to reconcile them. Steering the reader in opposite directions, Fisher's introduction does the novel a disservice. Writing to Aswell several years later about a preface to *Black Boy* (the proposed title at the time was *American Hunger*), Wright commented: "I'm wondering if the reader himself will not make up his mind as to what I'm trying to do when he is wading into the book?"[36] The question is equally relevant to *Native Son*.

4

Wright's novel was born, then, with the assistance of various white midwives, male and female. However much domesticated by white assistance at its delivery, it was still a robust infant whose loud cries reverberated through the literary atmosphere as the decade of the forties began. By presenting Bigger as he was — "resentful toward whites, sullen, angry, ignorant, emotionally unstable, depressed and unaccountably elated at times, and unable even, because of his own lack of inner organization which American oppression has fostered in him, to unite with members of his own race"[37] — Wright knew that he risked confirming in white minds a racist stereotype, that his own comrades in the Communist Party might reject his complex emotional and artistic honesty, and that the black bourgeoisie would be shamed by his frankness and would urge him to accentuate the positive in his racial portrayal. In a real sense, then, Wright was not so much appealing to

his audiences as he was confronting them with a harsh and un-
palatable truth, forcing them to undergo such emotional turmoil
as to cause them to reexamine their attitudes and expand their
awareness of the meaning, universally existential and politically
revolutionary as well as racially revealing, of Bigger Thomas.
Wright would assault his readers' sensibilities, not curry their favor
or indulge their sentimentality.

How well did he succeed? If there is one common denominator
of the 423 reviews, notices, essays, lectures, sermons, editorials,
letters to the editor, and poems that appeared in the two years after
the publication of the novel, it is their testimonial to the *power* of
the work, the searing emotional force that gripped readers with or
against their will. "Shock our sensibilities," "tremendous wallop,"
"power and drama and truth," "throbs from the opening line, with
a wallop propelled to the end," "tremendous power," "a terrible
story, a horrible story," "its frank brutalities . . . will horrify many
readers," "powerful story," "powerful novel," "engrossing, terrible
story," "a super-shocker," "grim and frightening," "one of the
most powerful novels of all time"[38] – such phrases occurred many
scores of times in the reviews of *Native Son*. So powerful was its
impact that one reviewer could only describe it as "a book which
takes you by the ears and gives you a good shaking, whirls you on
your toes and slaps you dizzy against the wall."[39] When the reader
regained full consciousness, one supposes, he or she could then
ponder the message Wright had conveyed with such overpowering
force.

Doing so, the reader was likely to note the thematic issues of race
and politics and the literary qualities of narration and characterization. Whatever its universal dimensions, *Native Son* is first of all a
novel about the American racial situation, and this aspect of its
theme elicited comment from almost all of its reviewers. For most,
regardless of race or region, Wright made a cogent as well as a
moving case against white racism. As far north as Maine an anon-
ymous reviewer noted that Bigger was a victim of environmental
determinism: "a mean Negro who might have been a solid asset in
another environment." As far south as Houston another claimed
that "Wright makes a masterful, unrelenting appeal" for racial
understanding, however much other southerners may object to

the novel's theme. In the Midwest a reviewer judged that "the picture of the Negro, against the white world, as presented by Wright, is the most illuminating I have ever read," and in California students emphasized its importance as a revelation of social injustice and a demand for change.[40] In the black press, reviews, editorials, and letters to the editor praising Wright's racial theme appeared in the *New York Amsterdam News, Kansas City Call, Chicago Metropolitan Post, The Chicago Defender, The New York Age, The Afro-American* (Baltimore), *The Philadelphia Tribune,* and other newspapers as well as in such important periodicals as *The Crisis, Phylon,* and *The Journal of Negro History.*[41] There were, of course, dissenters from this consensus. Many feared that Bigger was so unrepresentatively brutish that he would shame blacks and alienate whites. A lively debate on this subject appeared in *The Afro-American* (Baltimore) and *The Philadelphia Tribune,* as it also figured prominently in Communist discussions of the novel. A similar opinion was expressed by only a few nonradical white reviewers. Joseph McSorley feared that the "bestial, treacherous, utterly unlovable" Bigger would only stimulate more white oppression, and William E. Gilroy made a similar point. Wilbur Needham gave the controversy an interesting turn when he argued that instead of confirming racist stereotypes, Bigger's characterization was weak because it represented "the sort of Negro who had absorbed all white vices and retained none of the Negro virtues."[42] Many white southern reviews were surprisingly sympathetic to Wright's racial thesis – for example, those in *The Alabama Baptist, The Augusta Chronicle,* the *Charleston News and Courier, The Dallas Morning News,* the *Louisville Courier-Journal,* and the Memphis *Commercial Appeal* – but others expressed reservations or hostility, including the Jacksonville *Florida Times-Union, Fort Worth Star-Telegram, The Galveston News, Chattanooga Sunday Times,* and *The Times-Picayune New Orleans States.* In a national periodical, David L. Cohn of Mississippi, a writer of sorts himself, called the novel "a blinding and corrosive study in hate" and advised black people to emulate the patience of the Jews. Cohn was outdone by a white northern reviewer, Burton Rascoe, who considered the social message both obtrusive and erroneous.[43]

Rascoe's political preferences were involved in his extreme hostility to Wright's book, as indicated by his later accusation that as a Communist Wright was deliberately inciting racial hatred.[44] Other reviewers also voiced objections to the "warped ideology" which attempted "to make the Communist party seem the friend of the Negro."[45] The *Des Moines Sunday Register,* the *Newark Sunday Call,* and the *St. Louis Globe-Democrat* were especially blunt in their criticism of Wright's politics, and *The State* (Columbia, South Carolina) even went so far as to speak of the work's "strong odor of Communist and Negro propaganda."[46] Other anticommunist reviewers capitalized on Wright's treatment of the Jan–Mary–Bigger relationship, called by *Time* magazine "one of the most devastating accounts yet printed of that tragicomic, Negrophilous bohemianism which passes among Communists as a solution of the Negro problem."[47] In the other camp, Communists themselves debated the merits of the novel and its political implications, with influential spokesmen on both sides but the prevailing opinion favorable to Wright.[48] One of the most thoughtful political analyses of the novel was by a Trotskyite who emphasized Bigger's self-realization through revolutionary struggle but warned Wright about the Stalinists.[49] Finally, one might note the inevitable white liberals who congratulated themselves and the country on the book's publication and Wright's success. The rabbi of Temple Israel in New York cited this evidence of "the fact that here in our democracy we do not study a man's blood cells to evaluate genius but merely his creative ability," and *Newsweek,* admitting white responsibility for Bigger's plight, consoled itself that "in our system of government" such a book "can be openly printed, discussed, and answered."[50]

Concerning the strictly literary qualities of the novel, discussion centered around narration and characterization, with only a few perceptive observers noting Wright's symbolism. A clear consensus of praise for the work's literary artistry emerged, even from many who objected to its themes. Repeatedly the driving narrative momentum with its strong dramatic quality was singled out for favorable comment: "For the first two-thirds of the book," an influential midwestern reviewer wrote, "no tale of pursuit and capture has rivaled it."[51] Likewise, Wright's characterization, especially of Bigger, was widely admired, many reviewers agreeing with Henry

Seidel Canby's early comment that "only a Negro could have written"[52] such a psychologically penetrating book. Canby and a few others, indeed, seemed to emphasize the psychological dimension of Wright's story as a way of evading the social message. But more often reviewers considered characterization as well as narrative pace and structure as a means of realizing the author's theme. Many agreed with a reviewer in Albany, New York: "He has proven with this vigorous novel that for psychological imagination, for power of dramatic construction, for the convincingness and reality of his characters, he has few equals."[53] Reviewers who noted Wright's symbolism, his crisp dialogue, his "prose . . . as firm as steel,"[54] and his satiric touches helped to amplify the artistic particulars of the craft that had produced such a powerful effect.

In assessing this achievement, reviewers inevitably compared Wright to other writers, most frequently to Steinbeck, whose *The Grapes of Wrath* had appeared the year before; to Dostoevsky, author of another psychologically acute story of crime and punishment; and to Dreiser, author of another American tragedy. Several reviewers likened Wright to such socially conscious novelists as Erskine Caldwell, Charles Dickens, James T. Farrell, Maxim Gorky, and Harriet Beecher Stowe. Other writers, religious leaders, and a single filmmaker mentioned a time or two included Arna Bontemps, Millen Brand, Joyce Cary, Humphrey Cobb, Pietro di Donato, Thomas Dixon, Dos Passos, Dumas, Faulkner, Jessie Fauset, the Greek tragedians, D. W. Griffith, Hemingway, Victor Hugo, George Lee, Richard Llewellyn, Malraux, Albert Maltz, Claude McKay, Margaret Mitchell, Conrad Richter, Shakespeare, Upton Sinclair, Gertrude Stein, Tolstoy, Jean Toomer, Turgenev, Waters E. Turpin, Carl Van Vechten, Len Zinberg, Zola, Abraham Lincoln, the Biblical Samson, and Jesus Christ. However singular Wright's novelistic vision may have been, it was immediately placed by reviewers in various literary traditions, most notably that of social protest.

Native Son very quickly became a popular as well as critical success. Advance sales, Book-of-the-Month Club distribution, and first-week sales totaled 215,000 copies, an extremely large printing for a first novel. In its issue of March 16, 1940, two weeks after publication, *The Publishers' Weekly* alerted the book trade to high rates of reorders from bookstores and to Harper's heavy advertising campaign. An advertisement entitled "Public Stampedes for 'Native Son' " that appeared in various black newspapers was only mildly hyperbolical.[55] On the national best-seller charts, the novel first appeared in the second week of March, ranked very high though never in first place (a position held by Richard Llewellyn's *How Green Was My Valley*) for two months thereafter, began to fade in late spring, wilted in July, and did not appear in August or thereafter. In particular cities in particular weeks – New York, Chicago, Philadelphia, San Francisco, St. Louis – *Native Son* did rise to the top of the best-seller list.[56] Moreover, library copies were circulated briskly, although at least one library in a major southern city refused to purchase the book.[57]

Literary America was not yet ready to award a black writer a major prize in fiction, but the frequency with which Wright was nominated was another indication of the strong impact of *Native Son*. Only a few days after publication, the widely read columnist Franklin P. Adams penned the following versified "Book Review": "All the prizes should be won / By Richard Wright's 'Native Son.' " Soon afterward black journalists expressed similar sentiments, with Frank Marshall Davis predicting a Pulitzer Prize and Arthur Huff Fauset an eventual Nobel Prize for Wright. By May, such diverse voices as Walter Winchell and an editorial writer for *New Masses* had joined the chorus,[58] though ultimately to no avail. Still, *Native Son* was a serious contender for a Pulitzer Prize.

Another measure of the novel's effect is the way it was used in discussions of the actual social conditions reflected so graphically in the fictional work. Several journalists and sociologists cited *Native Son* in discussions of poor housing in Chicago and elsewhere.[59] Others drew parallels between Bigger Thomas and actual living individuals.[60] A writer in the denominational organ of the Disciples of Christ suggested that *Native Son* "would be a good book for all judges, police officers, and prosecutors who have to do with the Negro to read."[61]

It is always difficult to gauge precisely the effect of a problem novel on the future of the problem it treats, but from the available evidence it seems safe to claim that Wright's intention to shock his readers into a new awareness of the terrible dimensions of American racism was to a large degree accomplished. Irving Howe once wrote that "the day *Native Son* appeared, American culture was changed forever."[62] The change was not basic or profound, but it was real. The several hundred thousand readers of the work could no longer see racial issues in quite the same way. *Native Son* did not start a war, as Lincoln claimed *Uncle Tom's Cabin* did, or directly effect legislation, as *The Jungle* did, but it did alter the social as well as literary sensibilities of many of its readers.

5

It also had a profound effect on the course of black literature. A whole generation of black writers followed Wright's lead. Such first novels as Carl Offord's *The White Face* (1943), Chester Himes's *If He Hollers Let Him Go* (1945), Curtis Lucas's *Third Ward Newark* (1946), Ann Petry's *The Street* (1946), Alden Bland's *Behold a Cry* (1947), Willard Motley's *Knock on Any Door* (1947), William Gardner Smith's *The Last of the Conquerors* (1948), and Lloyd Brown's *Iron City* (1951) all work Wright's vein of naturalistic protest, through none achieve the other dimensions of *Native Son*. So pervasive was Wright's influence that it induced considerable anxiety in the two most gifted of his younger contemporaries, Ralph Ellison and James Baldwin, both of whom felt it necessary to slay their literary father, or at least distance themselves from what they understood to be his literary mode and his understanding of Afro-American culture. In his review of *Black Boy*, in his exchange with Irving Howe, and in numerous interviews, Ellison has felt compelled to repudiate Wright's literary paternity in order to assert his own literary identity, one which purports to go beyond Wrightian social protest.[63] The same can be said with even greater emphasis about James Baldwin. Wright helped the unknown Baldwin win a fellowship in 1945, only to be repaid a few years later with attacks on his work — especially the characterization of Bigger Thomas — in Baldwin's essays "Everybody's Protest Novel" and "Many Thousands Gone." If Ellison and Baldwin now seem expressive of the complacency of the fifties, a more militant mood among black writers revived in the sixties. In 1967 more than half of the thirty-eight writers polled by *Negro Digest* selected Wright as the foremost Afro-American author.[64]

At the same time academic interest in Wright and *Native Son* was developing rapidly, with books by Constance Webb, Edward Margolies, Dan McCall, Russell Brignano, Keneth Kinnamon, and David Bakish appearing in the late sixties and early seventies. Michel Fabre's full-scale biography, *The Unfinished Quest of Richard Wright* (1973), draws on thorough research in unpublished materials to provide details of Wright's life and an interpretation of his dual role as fighter against racial injustice and seeker of transracial humanistic perspectives. During this period two collections on *Native Son* were compiled, Richard Abcarian's *Richard Wright's Native Son: A Critical Handbook* (1970) and Houston A. Baker, Jr.'s, *Twentieth Century Interpretations of Native Son* (1972), the latter reprinting landmark essays by George Kent and Donald B. Gibson. Another indication of Wright's increasing recognition was a conference on him at the University of Iowa in 1971.

Interest in *Native Son* has continued unabated in recent years, with especially interesting work done by Joyce A. Joyce, Robert J. Butler, and James A. Miller. The highly successful international symposium on Wright at the University of Mississippi late in 1985 imparted additional impetus to work on the author. Moving beyond the old debate between protest and art, recent commentary on *Native Son*, often informed by new critical theory and perspectives, reveals previously unsuspected depth, complexity, and resonance in Wright's vision of black life and his literary resources in expressing it. The four essays which follow, appearing a half-century after the publication of *Native Son*, attest to its continuing power and fascination. Concerned with what he calls "the politics of literary representation," John M. Reilly shows how carefully Wright utilizes narrative techniques to subvert conventional American racial discourse and to establish the authority and authenticity of Bigger's voice. In "Native Sons and Foreign Daughters," Trudier Harris explores some of the social ironies involved in the novel's unfavorable presentation of female characters. As Bigger, responding to the American cultural values of individualism and freedom, aspires to soar, his mother, sister, and lover attempt to hold him down in the subservient place designated by the society as appropriate for black people. Houston A. Baker, Jr., focuses precisely on the concept of place in a new historicist treatment of black male and female roles in *Native Son* against the background of Wright's own interpretation of Afro-American history in *12 Million Black Voices*. The resulting indictment of Bigger and endorsement of Bessie complements the Harris essay while challenging much received opinion about Wright's protagonist. Finally, Craig Werner convincingly relates *Native Son* to modernism as a literary movement. Alienated and inarticulate, Bigger repeatedly struggles to tell as well as understand his story, becoming in the process a bluesy modernist black hero in a racist wasteland.

After making his claim that *Native Son* changed American culture, Irving Howe goes on to speak of "its crudeness, melodrama and claustrophobia of vision," implying that these literary defects somehow enhanced the power of the social statement. Considered together, the essays gathered here demonstrate that the social meaning of *Native Son*, whether or not one assents to it, emerges from its sophisticated literary technique, intricate psychological drama, and amplitude of vision. Readers of the novel should pay equal attention to its themes and its form. Doing so, whatever they may think of the changes Edward Aswell persuaded Wright to make, they must honor this editor for his prophetic confidence in the stature of *Native Son*. On February 29, 1940, the day before its publication, he wrote these words to Richard Wright: "I hope that this will reach you tomorrow, because I should like to be among the first to congratulate you once more on *Native Son*. You know what I think of it, and I have always thought of it, but let me be a little more explicit. It is not only a good book, a sincere, straight, and honest book, a courageous book, a powerful and eternally moving book, but in addition to all this, I truly believe, a great book. It is my conviction that its publication will be remembered in years to come as a monumental event." The present volume is offered as a token of such remembrance.

NOTES

1. For notices of the lectures cited see "Symposium on Negro Culture Today," *Daily Worker*, February 11, 1939, p. 7; "Wright Speaks Tonight

on Negro Culture," *Daily Worker*, May 12, 1939, p. 3; "Ford, Wright, Hughes to Speak at Savoy Sept. 2," *The Chicago Defender*, September 2, 1939, p. 24; printed invitation in the Wright Archive in the Beinecke Library at Yale; and "Wright Shows New Book," *The Chicago Defender*, February 24, 1940, p. 22.

2. "Book Marks for Today," *New York World-Telegram*, March 12, 1940, p. 17; "Richard Wright Tells Library Forum How He Wrote 'Native Son,'" *The New York Age*, March 16, 1940, p. 2; "'Native Son' Author to Relate Birth of 'Bigger,'" *The Chicago Defender*, July 6, 1940, p. 6; "'Native Son' Author Says Slump Wrecked Illusions," *Durham Morning Herald*, July 29, 1940, p. 3; Harry Hansen, "The First Reader," *New York World-Telegram*, September 9, 1940, p. 17.

3. Letters from Edward Aswell to Richard Wright dated May 12, June 13, June 18, and June 21, 1940, in the Wright Archive in the Beinecke Library.

4. Richard Wright, *How "Bigger" Was Born* (New York: Harper, 1940), p. 6.

5. Ibid., pp. 11, 11–12.

6. *American Hunger* (New York: Harper, 1977), p. 66. Originally the final third of the autobiographical manuscript completed late in 1943, this account of Wright's Chicago period was omitted when *Black Boy* was published in 1945, though portions had appeared in periodicals.

7. Wright, *How "Bigger" Was Born*, pp. 18, 26.

8. Ibid., pp. 29–30.

9. Letter of this date from Wright to his literary agent, Paul R. Reynolds, quoted by Michel Fabre in *The Unfinished Quest of Richard Wright* (New York: William Morrow, 1973), p. 556. Fabre's valuable treatment of the composition of *Native Son* (pp. 169–77) is based mainly on his correspondence with Jane Newton, who witnessed it at first hand.

10. Charles Leavelle, "Brick Slayer Is Likened to Jungle Beast," *Chicago Sunday Tribune*, June 5, 1938, Sec. 1, p. 6. Cf. *Native Son* (New York: Harper, 1940), pp. 238–40 [260–1]. References to *Native Son* throughout this volume will be made parenthetically. For the reader's convenience, bracketed page references to the paperback Perennial Classic edition will also be provided.

11. Margaret Walker Alexander, "Richard Wright," in David Ray and Robert M. Farnsworth, eds., *Richard Wright: Impressions and Perspectives* (Ann Arbor: University of Michigan Press, 1973), p. 60. In this important essay, Walker also relates Wright's visit to Chicago in November.

12. The complete agenda, to be found in the Wright Archive at Yale (JWJ Wright 813), follows:

1. Get detail map of the South Side. Street Car grades & maps
II. Pick out site for Dalton's home.
3. Get a good street layout for Dalton's home.
4. Select empty house for Bigger's murder of Bessie.
5. Trace with ample notes the legal route whch [sic] was taken in trying Nixon.
6. Go through Cook County Jail; get some dope from the project about it.
7. Get picture, if possible, and go through court where trial took place.
8. Select site for Blum's delicatessen.
9. Select area of Bigger's capture.
10. See, visit, death house at Statesville and talk to Nixon if possible.
11. Give Bessie's home a definite address.
12. (Detail execution, if possible (SEE).
13. Talk to ILD heads about pleas, court procedure. (Ira Silber)
14. Get from Chicago Public Library *Maureen's* book on Loeb and Leopold trial.
15. Get location of Loeb and Leopold and Franks old home
16. Get other books from library pertaining to trial
17. Investigate House of Correction for Boys.
18. Get complete dope on inquest.
19. Get a copy of inquest return verdict.
20. Get copy of indictments.
21. Get form in which judges [sic] sentence is rendered.
22. From what station would one go to Milwaukee on train?
23. Get "Old Rugged Cross" song for use in preacher's talk with Bigger.
24. Select site for Bigger's home (3700 block on Indiana). Investigate Indiana from 43 to 39 for scene of Bigger's capture.

13. For a different view of Max's politics, see Paul N. Siegel, "The Conclusion of Richard Wright's *Native Son,*" *PMLA* 89 (May 1974): 517–23.
14. I have also treated the Nixon case and its relation to *Native Son* in "*Native Son*: The Personal, Social, and Political Background," *Phylon* 30 (Spring 1969): 68–71, and *The Emergence of Richard Wright: A Study in Literature and Society* (Urbana: University of Illinois Press, 1972), pp. 121–5.

15. Wright, *How "Bigger" Was Born*, p. 39.
16. The revised page proofs at the Fales Collection of the New York University Library carry the date December 1, 1939.
17. Charles T. Davis and Michel Fabre's *Richard Wright: A Primary Bibliography* (Boston: G. K. Hall, 1982) is an invaluable guide to the study of Wright's texts, but it errs in calling the Schomburg version a "setting typescript" (p. 27). It is the first typed draft of 576 pages, for it contains opening and closing scenes dropped when the novel was set for galley proofs.
18. See the intermediate version in the Wright Archive at Yale, JWJ Wright 814. The passage appears on p. 61 [71] of the novel.
19. Wright Archive, JWJ Wright 814.
20. Wright Archive, JWJ Wright 954.
21. Wright Archive, JWJ Wright 813. Cf. *Native Son*, pp. 240, 241 [262, 263]. Apostrophes were added by an editor, not by Wright.
22. This scene and the original closing scene are in the Schomburg typescript of the first draft.
23. Wright, *How "Bigger" Was Born*, p. 38.
24. Ibid., p. 37.
25. Wright Archive, JWJ Wright 813.
26. Richard Wright, *Uncle Tom's Children* (New York: Harper, 1938), p. 314.
27. Henry F. Winslow's "Nightmare Experiences," *The Crisis* 66 (February 1959): 120–2, is a review of *The Long Dream* containing a pioneering discussion of fire imagery in Wright's work.
28. Reynolds's letters are in the Wright Archive at Yale.
29. Wright Archive, JWJ Wright 818.
30. The following deleted passage would have appeared in the first paragraph on p. 322 [351]: "A man whom Bigger recognized as the manager of the Regal Theatre told how Bigger and the boys like him masturbated in the theatre, and of how he had been afraid to speak to them about it, for fear they might start a fight and cut him."
31. It could also be the hand of Frances Bauman, who, according to Fabre, helped Wright go over the galleys. See *The Unfinished Quest of Richard Wright*, p. 177.
32. Wright Archive, JWJ Wright 813.
33. Letters from Edward Aswell to Richard Wright dated January 2, 11, and 18, 1940.
34. Robert B. Stepto, *From Behind the Veil: A Study of Afro-American Narrative* (Urbana: University of Illinois Press, 1979), pp. 3–31.
35. Stepto, *From Behind the Veil*, p. 129.

36. Letter from Richard Wright to Edward Aswell dated January 14, 1944, Box 34 of the Harper & Brothers Collection, Princeton University Library. Fisher was chosen instead of Wright to provide the introduction to *Black Boy* as well!

37. Wright, *How "Bigger" Was Born*, p. 21.

38. "*Afro* Readers Write About 'Native Son,'" *The Afro-American* (Baltimore), June 1, 1940, p. 13; "Among Books Reviewed in March *Boston Evening Transcript* Especially Recommends," *Boston Evening Transcript*, April 13, 1940, Sec. 5, p. 1; "Highlights in New Books," *The Bakersfield Californian*, March 26, 1940, p. 18; "'Native Son' Delves Into Race Problems," *The Sunday Pantagraph* (Bloomington, Illinois), March 10, 1940, p. 9 (this Associated Press review appeared in several other newspapers); "Negro's Answer," *Newsweek*, March 4, 1940, p. 40; "A Remarkable Book by Negro," *The Hartford Courant*, March 3, 1940, Magazine Sec., p. 6; "Wright, Richard. Native Son," *The Booklist* 36 (1 April 1940): 307; "Wright, Richard. Native Son," *Pratt Institute Library Quarterly Booklist* (October 1940): 24; A. M. F., "A Powerful Novel of Negro's Struggle in a White World," *Milwaukee Journal*, March 3, 1940, Part V, p. 3; Helen K. Fairall, "An Engrossing, Terrible Story Is This Novel About a Negro by a Negro," *Des Moines Register*, March 3, 1940, p. 9; Lewis Gannett, "Books and Things," *New York Herald Tribune*, March 1, 1940, p. 17; James Gray, "A Disturbing View of Our Unsolved Race Problem," *St. Paul Dispatch*, March 8, 1940, p. 10; W. L., "Another 'American Tragedy,'" *The News and Observer* (Raleigh), March 24, 1940, Sec. M., p. 5.

39. Bennett Davis, "Books of the Week in Review," *Buffalo Courier-Express*, March 3, 1940, Sec. 6, p. 2.

40. "Books and Bookfolk," *Portland Press Herald*, March 9, 1940, p. 13; "Negro's Novel Is Overwhelming, Bitter, Profound," *The Houston Press*, March 22, 1940, p. 27; "Powerful Plea for Negro Race," *Akron Beacon Journal*, March 10, 1940, p. 8-D; Barbara Ball, "The Vicarious World," Berkeley *Daily Californian*, March 26, 1940, p. 4; Dalton, "First Novel Wins Acclaim for Young Negro Writer," *The Stanford Daily*, April 10, 1940, p. 4.

41. For a survey of nearly all printed black reactions to the novel in 1940, see my "The Black Response to *Native Son*," forthcoming in a festschrift for the late Charles T. Davis edited by Kimberly W. Benston and Henry Louis Gates.

42. "Native Son. By Richard Wright," *The Catholic World* 151 (1940): 243; "What Will Be Its Effect?" *Advance* 132 (1940): 242, 274; "Negro

Author Pens Story of Racial Relationships," *Los Angeles Times*, March 10, 1940, Part III, p. 7.

43. "The Negro Novel: Richard Wright," *The Atlantic Monthly*, May 1940, p. 659; "Negro Novel and White Reviewers," *The American Mercury*, May 1940, pp. 113–16. Wright responded in print to both of these reviews.

44. "Do Critics Help?" *The American Mercury*, August 1940, pp. 502–3.

45. John Selby, "The Literary Guidepost," *Ashland Daily Independent*, March 3, 1940, p. 4. This syndicated review appeared in at least eighteen other newspapers.

46. Helen K. Fairall, "An Engrossing, Terrible Story Is This Novel About a Negro by a Negro," *Des Moines Register*, March 3, 1940, p. 9; "Exploring the Book World," *Newark Sunday Call*, March 3, 1940, Part III, p. 5; James E. Daughtery, "Powerful Novel of Negro Life," *St. Louis Globe-Democrat*, March 9, 1940, p. 18; Murray de Q. Bonnoitt, "Under the Covers," *The State* (Columbia, South Carolina), August 18, 1940, p. 5-B.

47. "'Bad Nigger,'" *Time*, March 4, 1940, p. 72. Among reviews making the same point, see especially F. A. Breyer, "Young Black Man's Nemesis," *The Cincinnati Enquirer*, March 2, 1940, p. 5; and Ted Robinson, "*Native Son*. By Richard Wright," *Cleveland Plain Dealer*, March 10, 1940, All Feature Sec., p. 3.

48. See my *The Emergence of Richard Wright*, pp. 147–50.

49. J. R. Johnson, "Native Son and Revolution," *The New International*, May 1940, pp. 92–3. James T. Farrell attacked what he considered Wright's Stalinism in "Farrell Throws Brickbats at Saroyan, Fante, Wright, Maltz, di Danto [sic], Weidman and Brand – Merry Xmas," *The Chicago Daily News*, December 4, 1940, p. 39.

50. William F. Rosenblum, "Some Notable Comment on *Native Son*," in *Native Son*, "Seventh Edition" (New York: Harper, 1940), p. 368; "Negro's Answer," *Newsweek*, March 4, 1940, p. 41.

51. Fanny Butcher, "Negro Writes Brilliant Novel, Remarkable Both as Thriller and a Psychological Record," *Chicago Daily Tribune*, March 6, 1940, p. 19.

52. "Native Son by Richard Wright," *Book-of-the-Month Club News*, February 1940, pp. 2–3.

53. R. J. L. [ewis], Jr., "Between the Book Covers," Albany *Times-Union*, March 3, 1940, p. 10A.

54. Lee Berry, "The World of Books," *Toledo Blade*, March 9, 1940, p. 5.

55. "Book Marks for Today," *New York World-Telegram*, March 12, 1940, p.

17; "'Native Son' Sells Rapidly," *The Publishers' Weekly* 137 (1940): 1161; *New York Amsterdam News*, March 9, 1940, p. 2; *The New York Age*, March 16, 1940, p. 2; *The Pittsburgh Courier*, March 23, 1940, p. 4, and several subsequent issues through May 11, 1940.

56. I base this information on charts in the *Brooklyn Eagle*, *The New York Times*, *New York Herald Tribune Books*, and *The Publishers' Weekly.*

57. "News of Books and Authors," *Daily Worker*, July 15, 1940, p. 7; Angelo Herndon, "Books Read at Harlem Library Show People Seek a Way Out of Poverty," *Sunday Worker*, April 7, 1940, p. 5. On the banning in Birmingham, see "Dixie Library Bans 'Native Son': Alabama Library Won't Place 'Native Son' on Its Shelves," *The Pittsburgh Courier*, April 20, 1940, pp. 1, 4; letters to the editor of *The Birmingham News* on March 17, 22, 30, 31, and April 5, 12, 14, 1940; the editorial "Banning Books Indirectly," *The Birmingham News*, April 5, 1940, p. 16; letters to the editor of *The Birmingham Post* on March 16, 20, and April 2, 10, 1940; the editorial "Throwing No Stone," *The News and Observer* (Raleigh), April 1, 1940, p. 4; and Lillian E. Smith, "Dope with Lime," *The North Georgia Review*, Spring 1940, mimeographed letter, p. 1.

58. F.[ranklin] P. A.[dams], "The Conning Tower," *New York Post*, March 4, 1940, p. 14; "'Native Son' Greatest Novel Yet by American Negro," *The Nashville Defender*, March 9, 1940; "I Write as I See: A Negro Renaissance?" *The Philadelphia Tribune*, April 4, 1940, p. 4; Walter Winchell, "On Broadway," New York *Sunday Mirror*, May 5, 1940, p. 10; "Pulitzer Awards," *New Masses*, May 14, 1940, p. 26.

59. "Chicago Slum Shown in Negro Writer's Novel," *Public Housing Weekly News*, April 9, 1940, p. 2; Horace R. Cayton, "Negro Housing in Chicago," *Social Action* 6 (1940): 4–38; Arthur E. Holt, "The Wrath of the Native Son," *The Christian Century* 57 (1940): 570–2; Frank L. Hayes, "Murder Motive in Book Traced to Housing Evil," *The Chicago Daily News*, May 6, 1940, p. 11; Michael Carter, "244,000 Native Sons," *Look*, May 21, 1940, pp. 8–13; Samuel Harkness, "Some Notable Comment on *Native Son*," in *Native Son*, "Seventh Edition," pp. 363–4; I. F. Stone, "The Rat and Res Judicata," *The Nation*, November 23, 1940, pp. 495–6.

60. "Native Son Used to Halt an Eviction," *The Chicago Defender*, May 11, 1940, national edition, pp. 1–2; Sam Lacy, "Wright's Novel Comes True: Washington's 'Native Son' Blames Poverty for Life of Crime," *Washington Afro-American*, June 1, 1940, p. 5; "Conditions Breed 'Bigger Thomas'; Bring Terror and Violence to Community," *New York Amsterdam News*, September 14, 1940, p. 10.

61. C. W. Lemmon, "Book Chat," *World Call,* May 1940, pp. 23, 46.
62. "Black Boys and Native Sons," *Dissent* 10 (1963): 354.
63. See especially Ralph Ellison, *Shadow and Act* (New York: New American Library, 1966).
64. Hoyt W. Fuller, "A Survey: Black Writers' Views on Literary Lions and Values," *Negro Digest* 17 (January 1968): 10–48, 81–9.

2

Giving Bigger a Voice: The Politics of Narrative in *Native Son*

JOHN M. REILLY

To a greater extent than we usually care to admit, our reading of a novel like *Native Son* has been framed by prior experiences that urge us to anticipate, even to seek, confirmation of information we already possess. Its character may be vastly different for us today than it was for readers fifty years ago, when *Native Son* became the first work by a black American author to reach the best-seller list, but despite the evidence that the book reached a large biracial audience in 1940 and continues to do so today, there is reason to believe that readers are unprepared to appreciate how much real news *Native Son* will bring them.

The first-time reader of *Native Son* may be said to be unacquainted with Bigger Thomas and unaware of the direction the plot of the novel, his life's story, will take; however, the same thing can be said about a first reading of, say, a detective story. We do not yet know the traits of the sleuth, or the way the criminal puzzle will be solved. But we have a pretty good idea, because experience has taught us that by and large crime and mystery stories are about the same thing. It is anticipation of the secondary details of detection methods, setting, or ingenuity of plot that attracts us to read the newest thriller. The analogy between a detective novel and what the trade calls a straight novel is not precise, but it is serviceable enough to suggest that readers will approach *Native Son*, as they do any novel, with a lifetime's preparation, much of it as painlessly acquired as the ability to interpret the marks of printing on the page as signs evoking the structures and concepts of their native language. With a similar lack of awareness about the weight of cultural baggage it carries, an audience comes to *Native Son* with experience in the field of discourse on blacks in America. However extensive or limited their personal experience of racial variety may be, readers' minds are a repository of anecdotes, stereotypes, and remembered declarations, providing white readers a set of assumptions about Afro-Americans that will be applied as naturally to the novel as will their linguistic competence, and giving black readers a seemingly unending need to read any literature with caution to see if the record must be set straight once more. In either case, white or black, the reader will have experienced discourse about Afro-Americans that is typically advanced by reference to their difference from the socially dominant Euro-American standard of culture. In civilization, history, family patterns, language, art, psychology, the white is always the norm; the black is forever the "other."

It is not necessary to review the substance of these collectively held views, since the cluster of beliefs surrounding race pervades the popular mind as extensively as the American Creed. It is only pertinent to remark that like those convictions we commonly call myths, the consensual views about race are transmitted through the medium of language. The point may seem obvious, but it is worth a moment's reflection nevertheless. Everything we know about the past, for example, comes to us either through commentary on mute artifacts or by writings that preserve in their form and style somebody else's interpretation of events. All that we know about distant occurrences in our contemporary world arrives by oral accounts, selective photography, or written reportage. Even local happenings are shared largely by talk. All this should make it clear that most of what human beings know about reality is not gained from direct experience at all. Most of our knowledge comes to us already mediated, already freighted with a society's consensual values. Just as we are taught to see the significant features of a landscape in accordance with our culture's relative admiration of the wild or tamed elements of the physical environment, so are we instructed by the fund of writing and talk that is our collective legacy to measure human behavior. Whoever charts the landmarks also plots reality; whoever frames the discourse controls knowledge.

Social power expresses itself in monopoly upon the right to define meaning. Thus, on the obsessive American topic of race, the dominant population – those who chose to call themselves white in order to distinguish their status from that of the people whose slavery and subordination were justified on the basis of skin color – have accorded to themselves the right to compile the documents and relate the tales that define blackness, thereby controlling the circumstances of discussion while suppressing the humanity of the people objectified in stories and documents as "other." Of course, blacks have not been supine in the face of white power. They have created a vital, unique culture within the social, linguistic, and geographic boundaries of America; have contested the power of oppression through political or military action; and, as we shall soon see, have produced significant literature founded on premises different from those of white America. In the record of black resistance, *Native Son* has a special place as an instance of direct challenge to the power of prevailing discourse. It not only questions the factuality of received views, but also carries the challenge into the mechanisms of discourse itself with skill and artistry that give readers a great deal more news than they bargained for.

The success of the challenge rests first upon the paradox of unanticipated redundancy we have been discussing; readers enter the novel as though it were an entirely new treatment, while unconsciously bringing to bear on the narrative a fund of received lore. But there is another, related paradox that lies at the heart of Wright's strategic calculations in *Native Son*. This second paradox pertains to the premise of realism. As Ian Watt has explained, the novel classically works in the manner of circumstantial evidence, offering its descriptions as the particulars of a given case meant to persuade readers, like a jury, that a single, valid explanation will connect those particulars into a consecutive story. Even though the matter of a realistic novel is language rather than material evidence, the practice of realistic story-telling conceals the insubstantiality of words, so that they will be taken as concretely referential and allow us the pleasurable illusion of sharing "a full and authentic report of human experience."[1] Richard Wright takes advantage of this mimetic quality of narrative fiction to found his novel on a dense web of particularized details that simulate reality, luring readers to read his references not as the conventions that they are, but as the equivalent of actuality.

37

Street names, addresses (all located on the actual grid of Chicago's streets), descriptions of building exteriors, and passing references to such contemporary topical matters as the mass transportation system, the city's politics, neighborhood ethnicity, and the economics of tenement housing ownership — each of these helps to generate the conviction that the author knows first-hand the city that became a terminus for the massive southern black migration during the first decades of the twentieth century. Because the race of its author has always been widely publicized, readers probably sense additional veracity in these details as they realize *Native Son* draws upon Wright's own participation in the historical relocation of the peasantry to urban centers.

Certainly the evocation of social details in such passages as the novel's opening scene in the Thomas apartment does a great deal to advance the impression of Wright's special qualifications to report the authentic life of impoverished black migrants to Chicago. At the same time that the episode of Bigger's killing of the rat foreshadows later violence, it also has the intrinsic significance of an abstract of ghetto life where health, comfort, convenience, and security are impossible because the relief system will not provide the means; and family coherence, nurture, and affection have been so eroded that family members have become atomized individuals rather than a kinship group combining their resources for survival and growth. Because realistic fiction ordinarily recounts the career of a remarkable individual in such a way as to make the novel comparable to a biographical memoir, it is not unusual to minimize the effect of the protagonist's family lineage; but Wright's introduction of Bigger within an atomized family has quite another effect. Instead of making him attractively solitary, a potentially heroic overreacher, Wright's initial presentation of Bigger gives him definition as a figure tentatively singled out by the narrative as the focus of a microcosmic scene of the life of the South Side black underclass. In that sense he is from the start a representative native son.

Wright had a deep faith that the structures of social reality would permit characterization of Bigger as typical. One of the personal discoveries he made when he migrated to Chicago was the investigative method of social science. Several years after the publication of *Native Son* he testified to the importance of the generalized findings of social science in his introduction to the landmark study of Chicago's South Side by St. Clair Drake and Horace Cayton, *Black Metropolis*. Recalling his arrival in Chicago as a migrant seeking freedom, he wrote that the city presented him with "extremes of possibility, death and hope" while he "lived half hungry and afraid in a city to which I had fled with the dumb yearning to write, to tell my story."[2] There can be little doubt that Wright's intellectual eagerness and heroic drive to express himself would have led him to produce the literature he aspired to write regardless of circumstances. Nevertheless, here is how he described the critical contribution of social science to his career:

> I did not know what my story was, and it was not until I stumbled upon science that I discovered some of the meanings of the environment that battered and taunted me. I encountered the work of men who were studying the Negro community, amassing facts about urban Negro life, and I found that sincere art and honest science were not far apart, each could enrich the other.[3]

In the same essay Wright described the extent of that collaborative enrichment with specific reference to his first novel:

> If, in reading my novel, *Native Son*, you doubted the reality of Bigger Thomas, then examine the delinquency rates cited in this book . . . *Black Metropolis* describes the processes that make the majority of Negroes on Chicago's South Side sixth-graders, processes that make 65 per cent of all Negroes on Chicago's South Side earn their living by manual labor. After studying the social processes in this book, you cannot expect Negro life to be other than it is . . . The imposed conditions under which Negroes live detail the structure of their lives like an engineer outlining the blue-prints for the production of machines.[4]

Wright's insistence upon a correlation between his fiction and the findings of empirical research helps to recall the circumstances of a black writer in 1940. At other times also Wright was moved, as in the *Black Metropolis* essay, to tell his audience to seek verification of his fiction beyond its pages. To a second, expanded edition of his collection of short stories *Uncle Tom's Children*, originally published in 1938, he added an autobiographical essay about "The Ethics of Living Jim Crow," first published in 1937. The motive for appending a previously issued essay to the new edition of short stories was the same as that expressed in his introduction to *Black Metropolis* — to address directly those readers who found it difficult to believe that things were as bad as the devices of his fiction suggested. The problem Wright hoped to solve was the same vexed one of authority that had always preoccupied Afro-American written literature. During the nineteenth century it was common practice for editors and publishing firms to attach letters of testimony to narratives written by fugitive slaves. Dozens of those narratives were published; yet it seemed necessary to provide practically all of them with documentation indicating that though the evidence of literacy might suggest otherwise, the author had been in fact a slave, was indeed black, and that reported incidents in the narrative could be corroborated by recognizably trustworthy informants.[5] In the context of this tradition of a dubious readership, it is not surprising that following the publication of his novel Wright felt compelled to explain its genesis, both on the lecture platform and in print.[6] Evidently the need to establish the credentials of veracity for the black author remained as compelling in 1940 as it had been a century before.

In the light of this unique problem of authority that Wright faced, we can return to the *Black Metropolis* introduction. There, while Wright's autobiographical references to the importance of social science give insight into his sense of the practice of realism, he is also addressing the problem of securing a platform from which to mount a challenge to conventional views about Afro-Americans. Referring to Drake and Cayton's book, but also by extension to his own, he wrote:

> The authors know well that white Americans take it for granted that they know Negroes, and they understand why whites hold to their presumed knowledge with such fierceness. The authors know that the Negro has been on the American scene for some three hundred years, and has been in our society as a more or less free agent for more than seventy-five years. They know, too, that a book like *Black Metropolis* might come as a jolt to whites who assume that their knowledge of the Negro excels the knowledge of Negroes by Negroes. Some whites will feel that they had some special ax to grind.[7]

The presumptuous and smug readers to whom Wright refers resist the findings of social science because those findings conflict with the attitudes expressed in America's dominant discourse on race. The "truth" related in popular anecdote and racial bias seems truer than the reportage of Drake and Cayton, because theirs is the language of the "other," a classification that mutes contesting voices. If sociological writing can encounter such resistance, how much more difficult must be the job of creating an alternative discourse in the indeterminate realm of fiction.[8]

However accurate Wright made the realistic surface of *Native Son* and however strenuously he claimed support for his novel's authenticity in the findings of social science, he had to know that authority to speak about black experience is not exclusively a matter of knowledge. Authority in fiction, particularly fiction concerning a group denominated a "minority," is above all political, for the simple reason that monopoly of discourse is an integral part of the monopoly of social power. Long anecdotal and declarative repetition of the belief that a "nigger is a nigger" supports the social structures creating the subordinate group that can be slurred, while in turn the institutionalized structures of racism reflexively generate racist discourse as their justification.

To take up the challenge presented to him by the political configurations of American discourse on race, Richard Wright had to do more than create a narrative that would be recognizably accurate in its localized detail.[9] Since the problem was political, its solution lay in adoption of narrative techniques that would recreate the literary form of the social novel as a black text.

Ready to hand for the purpose was the model of a distinctive language practice in Black English whereby an innocuous statement outwardly conforming to conventional expectation carries within it a critical or satiric judgment offered from the perspective of the ostensibly powerless social subordinate. Related to literary irony, this technique of using signs — popularly called "signifying" — lends itself to stressing contradiction, as when tone of voice in such a statement as "Of course in America all men are created equal" underlines the divergence of actuality from ideal; to mockery, as when the speech habits of the dominant caste are exaggerated in the same manner as minstrel performers used to parade as dandies, carrying the finery and manners of the rich to an extreme; and to inversion of standards, as in the familiar attribution of positive reference to terms that in white usage have negative connotation – *black* may mean sinister in the white vernacular, but in the Afro-American world it has become honorific.[10] When Bigger and Gus play "white" in Book One of *Native Son* they are signifying, and in the process revealing that they have greater knowledge of the signs and gestures associated with status than anyone outside their community would be prepared to credit to them. The practical sociology underlying signifying becomes evident also when Bigger adjusts his answers and physical manner under interrogation by Britten because "he knew that whites thought that all Negroes yearned for white women," and "therefore he wanted to show a certain fearful deference when one's name was mentioned in his presence."[11]

Signifying makes abundantly clear the social determination of linguistic tactics. While all language is a social product, and instances of its usage always represent accommodation to an audience as well as adaptation to purposes not entirely self-evident, the Afro-American technique of indirection also resonates with indications of its origins among the people classified as "other." Whether embodied in calculatingly differential gesture or elaborated in the cycle of trickster tales about slaves who dupe their masters, the obliquity of signifying is never simply individual, because it is undertaken in the knowledge that the identity of the signifying speaker is presumed to derive primarily from membership in a subordinate race. If individuality is secondary to racial designation, one is necessarily spokesperson for the collective. The status may be relished, and it obviously can stimulate ingenious linguistic construction, but the circumstance of being always viewed first of all as black guarantees that one's language must be broadly political. Signifying is, thus, an example of creative politics that draws upon a store of knowledge about the ways of white folks to achieve ends that custom and prevalent racial assumptions deem improper. Those ends may be material, but inevitably they also have a great deal to do with the integrity of the signifying speaker, who by the subversive tactic of manipulating stereotypes achieves a clandestine subjectivity, the right to be a free human agent.

Beyond the incidents in which Bigger displays a knowledge of practical sociology in order to signify, the pertinence of Afro-American indirection and reversal of expectations appears in the system of characterization and exposition Wright selected for *Native Son*. Consider, for example, Bigger's antagonists. Britten and Buckley are depicted as complete racists, extreme in their sentiments and self-serving in their pursuit of Bigger; but they are secondary figures who become agents of the plot only when the mechanisms of criminal investigation and prosecution are set in motion. It is the Dalton family that first intervenes in Bigger's life, instigating the plot that leads to murder and Bigger's final fate – and the family's racism is not immediately evident. In fact each of the Daltons intends what is considered to be an improvement in Bigger's condition. Mr. Dalton's embarrassed suppression of the fact that he owns Bigger's squalid housing may arouse contempt, as does his boastful announcement of membership in the NAACP, but this behavior is no more villainous than is Mrs. Dalton's insensitive habit of ignoring Bigger's presence while she counsels her husband that they "inject him into his new environment at once" (p. 40 [48]). In other words, their responsibility for institutionalizing racism through the exploitation of their tenants and the enforcement of segregated housing patterns cannot be attributed directly to their characters, in the way that Britten and Buckley may be seen to be motivated by race hatred. Yet, as the logic of the novel shows, the Daltons' complicity in exploitation is a greater evil than the Klan-like behavior of Britten and Buckley, for their controlling role in the economic and social system of Chicago creates the conditions that frustrate and oppress not only the Thomases but all blacks in the city, conditions that in turn require the active reinforcement of the overt racism that the Daltons are too respectable to indulge, too self-deluded to acknowledge as necessary to the maintenance of their social position.

Had Wright omitted the elder Daltons from his narrative, he could have written a conventional story of allegorized evil and its helpless victim. By including them, however, and by gradually insinuating the ultimate responsibility of the Daltons for the course

43

of Bigger's life, Wright evades melodrama – which his readers would more than likely have received as special pleading – and balances the character of Bigger with figures who are representative of the system of oppression precisely because of their white normality.

The innovation in Wright's conception of Bigger's antagonists becomes bolder in the presentation of Mary Dalton. Perhaps she is a naive young woman when she invites Bigger to forget the learning of a lifetime and act as her social equal in segregated Chicago, but she is well-intentioned and more receptive than her parents to understanding how society is structured. Yet even though it is the accident of her birth rather than active complicity that involves her in the system of racial oppression, she is the Dalton who attracts Bigger's suppressed rage. She is the one who becomes the unlikely victim when Bigger enacts his persistent fantasy of blotting out the people who frustrate him. Why does Wright choose to make her the victim of a black man's murder?

One answer is thematic. Wright makes Bigger commit two apparently senseless murders, and the victims are women rendered relatively powerless in society by their gender or race. Each of them also seeks a personal relationship with Bigger that she expects can be maintained as an enclave of experience apart from the social reality of racism. Mary wants a color-blind acquaintanceship; Bessie wants an intimacy that releases spontaneous feeling. Both types of relationship are certainly desirable, and we may recognize that we usually view friendship and love just as Mary and Bessie do – as occurrences that are purely personal. In *Native Son* no such division of experience is possible, because it is Wright's intention to show that social conditions cannot be ameliorated by exclusively personal action. Just as his portrayal of Bigger's antagonists shows that racism is systemic and that Britten and Buckley are its agents rather than its source, so, too, his portrayal of the victims of Bigger's murders directs attention beyond the individuals. The oppression of racism makes no individual distinctions. The relegation of people to the miserable conditions of South Side Chicago, like the intellectual assumptions and stereotypes that characterize blacks as inferior, is an act visited upon a group without regard for any presumed difference between personal and social experience; and the response stimulated by oppression, Wright is telling his readers, will naturally enough be no more discriminating.

There is also a second reply to the question of why Wright chose to make Mary the victim of a black man's murder, this one phrased in the form of another question: why are readers inclined to be so critical of Mary Dalton that they come near to justifying Bigger's violence against her? The *Book-of-the-Month Club News,* announcing the selection of *Native Son* to its members in February 1940, described Mary as flighty and patronizing; one reviewer called her a dilettante-Communist; another saw her as part of "a terrible picture of the provocation the white race gives to black boys to misbehave"; yet another called her "dim-witted" and a "parlor red" who "fancies herself a Negrophile"; and *Time* magazine spoke of her "tragi-comic, Negrophilous bohemianism."[12] Curiously, even as they indulged their own racial and political biases, some of these reviewers were moved to imply that Mary had it coming to her. Obviously the reviewers missed Wright's point about the individuality of experience and, consequently, viewed Mary's murder in terms of personal motive alone. If we ask why reviewers of *Native Son* in 1940 – and surely more than a few recent readers – have found Mary so offensive that they tend to justify her death, we will reach the heart of Wright's narrative invention and the key element in his challenge to prevailing discourse about Afro-Americans.

It is not any failing in Mary's character that provokes an explanation of her murder that amounts to ascription of a justifiable personal motive to Bigger. Instead it is Wright's decision to use a narrative point of view closely identified with Bigger's, though not identical to it, that accounts for readers' taking his side. Closely associated with Bigger's thought and expository of his feelings, the presiding narrative voice blurs the color lines and gives readers – white and black – the sensations and perspective of an underclass character. The subtle narrative reports Bigger's thought and pre-conscious feeling in the language of third-person story-telling; but while maintaining the third-person reference, the narrative also suggests a simulation of the character's own mental discourse. That technique, known as "free indirect discourse," is not in itself unusual. When employed in the service of a character like Bigger,

however, it becomes a remarkable innovation in American realistic fiction, rarely matched before 1940 except by Mark Twain's
giving the frontier ruffian Huck Finn the right to tell his own story,
or by Theodore Dreiser's investment of subjectivity in working
women like Carrie Meeber. In the line of realism, from the frontier
sketches through the fiction of William Dean Howells and Stephen
Crane, when outsiders or bottom dogs such as frontier settlers,
immigrants, and ethnic characters appear, they are presented in a
frame story or through the mediation of a narrative voice firmly
middle-class in its language, taste, and orientation. Thus the frontier humor of the Old Southwest is often reported by a narrator
who comes from a metropolitan center, introducing an exotic
country person who is allowed to tell a story in dialect before the
reporter reestablishes his presence in standard English. Even the
city of New York can appear to be full of aliens in such a novel as
Howells's *A Hazard of New Fortunes*, which presents the industrial
working class as beyond the ken of the editor Basil March, who is
the focal point of the narrative, or Crane's *Maggie*, in which the
narrative voice reductively presents its Irish-American subjects
with hardly an indication that they even possess consciousness.
Each of these representative texts in the tradition of American
realism illustrates the habit of enforcing the perception shared by a
dominant class. By distancing the narrative from socially subordinate groups distinguished by strong differences in dialect or appearance, by withholding explanation of their behavior, and above
all by establishing a narrative viewpoint readily identifiable as old
stock, formally educated, and more learned than frontier settlers,
workers, and ethnics, these normative texts create an identification between readers and authors that expresses the monopoly
of discourse by a ruling caste or class. That monopoly is exactly
what Richard Wright aims to subvert in *Native Son* by use of a narrative point of view that draws readers beneath the externals of
surface realism, so that as they are led into empathy with Bigger,
they will be denied the conventional attitudes of American racial
discourse.

Departure from the narrative point of view that had become
conventional in mainstream American realism was a risky busi-
ness for Wright. For one thing, his use of richly denotative and

analytic language to project Bigger's feelings into the narrative might strike some readers as hardly realistic at all, since it cannot be assumed that Bigger himself would possess the same developed resources as his creator. One prominent reviewer, Burton Rascoe of the *American Mercury*, who found it impossible "to conceive of a novel's being worse, in the most important respects, than *Native Son*," centered his attention on what he understood to be self-evident literary guidelines, among which were such supposed rules as that if a character is inarticulate about conditions he should not be conscious of them, and that "it is a violation of aesthetic principle to portray characters behaving in a way not consistent with the way you the writer might conceivably do."[13] In effect, Rascoe was charging that Wright's selection of narrative point of view violated the premises of realism, but beneath the indictment lay an unspoken assumption deriving from stereotypical discourse on race – namely, the belief that a character such as Bigger who does not express himself in standard English will not have reached the level of reason that standard English is alleged to represent. Rascoe's second rule, proscribing the portrayal of behavior that an author himself would never conceivably exhibit in similar circumstances, states a doubt that social environment determines the formation of character. Again the critical stricture appears to derive from a supposition having more to do with racism than literature, this time the callous assumption that social conditions engendered by the system of white supremacy have no effects one must acknowledge, since persons of merit will rise in any case, just as Wright did. It is no wonder that this backhanded compliment lodged in a review that derogated his narrative experiment provoked Wright to take the extraordinary measure of writing a sharp answer which stressed his right to tell the truth as he knew it.[14]

A further risk run by Wright when he chose his narrative point of view is suggested by another contemporary review, this time a favorable one written by the poet Sterling Brown in *Opportunity*, the magazine issued by the Urban League. Noting with approval the revelatory description of setting in the novel and the thrilling conduct of narrative, Brown stated that the greatest achievement of *Native Son* was the character of Bigger Thomas:

It took courage to select as hero, a wastrel, a sneak thief, a double-killer. Most writers of minority groups select as heroes those who disprove stereotypes. Here is the "bad nigger" set down without squeamishness, doing all that the "bad nigger" is supposed to do.[15]

Brown does not elaborate the point in his review, but the "bad nigger" has a prominent place in Afro-American oral literature, where his flaunting of Jim Crow elevates him to the position of folk hero. The character of Bigger, whose badness also emerges in response to oppressive racial conditions, can be understood as a signifying trope providing black readers of *Native Son* a shock of recognition and opening for white readers access to the serious social meaning of the imaginative Afro-American literary tradition. For both groups in the dual audience the presence of the trope indicates Wright's further step toward making the form of the realistic novel a black vehicle.

This depends, however, on Wright's evading the possibility that his presentation of Bigger will either confirm the stereotype of the bestial Negro for readers who bring to the novel ideas about less-than-human inferiors, or substantiate the patronizing image of pitiable victim for those whose intellectual baggage includes an impulsive but self-protective sympathy for the underdog. Wright speaks to the latter danger in *How "Bigger" Was Born* when he presents his resolution to prohibit readers "the consolation of tears," an end he suggests accomplishing by the quasiscientific procedure of putting Bigger into certain situations and letting him work his way out according to the laws governing the environment. Yet despite the corroborative value in the testimony about a scientific approach, description of his narrative as though it were documentary reportage is neither accurate nor sufficient to meet the danger of confirming the negative stereotype. As Sterling Brown's review of *Native Son* indicated, the Afro-American fiction before Wright denied the stereotype by selecting protagonists whose traits were antithetical to racist characterization. Most commonly this meant that authors employed a tactic of attempting to evoke readers' appreciation of characters by displaying their conformity to norms shared with the white middle class, and, if the plot required these characters to meet a violent or otherwise sorry end, making their fate the arbitrary consequence of skin color and caste designation with no suggestion of conjunction between character, action, and fate. Obviously this conventional tactic of so-called minority literature was no more satisfactory to Wright's purposes than was the mainstream convention of establishing a narrative voice that does not enter into or describe the consciousness of underclass characters, for neither type of narration could challenge the substance of the American discourse on race. Shrewdly acceding to the appearance of realism by weaving a thick texture of particularized detail in order to authenticate the historicity of Bigger and his experience, and enticing the reader to expect novelty with the portrayal of Bigger as a dangerously confused young man, Wright meets the initial requirements of the contract between reader and author of realistic fiction. Providing verisimilitude, Wright allows the reader to accept the story's illusion as an imitation of reality and in return receives a chance to set a topic that will rectify the ignorance of the audience.

Inherent in the idea of a contract between author and reader is the fact that a novel is collaborative. Existing only as it is read, the novel makes writer and reader more or less equal partners – the reader's subjectivity becomes as significant as the objectification of the writer's imagination in the text. Of course, that is why communication about race is so problematic: the reader's subjectivity has been shaped by the preceding texts that make up the field of racial discourse. Yet, except in the case of the most dogmatic readers, the audience that participates in the writer's project by recovering the thought and feeling objectified in a narrative enters a community more free than other areas of life, a community where the decision to keep on turning the pages concedes validity to the text and its author's vision of life. It is within this dimension of his readers' experience that Richard Wright introduces a new contractual provision that allows him to make the personality of Bigger Thomas the central element of narrative.

Even while describing in his *Black Metropolis* essay how his book was founded on quantified data, Wright noted that social research made possible contemplation of new topics:

> For example, what peculiar personality formations result when millions of people are forced to live lives of outward submissiveness while trying to keep intact in their hearts a sense of the worth of

their humanity? What are the personality mechanisms that subli-
mate racial resentments which, if expressed openly, would carry
penalties varying from mild censure to death?[16]

The questions are ones he attempted to answer in *Native Son*, in
which Wright established Bigger's personality as the terrain where
environment and individuality meet to produce the subjectivity
unacknowledged either in the stereotypes retailed by racist discourse or in the traditional narrative modes of social fiction. Although for reasons already indicated Wright seized upon details
and concepts that would lend veracity to Bigger's story and wel-
comed the chance to confirm that veracity further with his extratextual commentary, Richard Wright made every effort to assure
that readers would not take *Native Son* as simply a restatement of
data, depending for its truth upon outside sources. He sought authority not for his facts but for his fiction. His finely tuned narrative
point of view shuns the externalized vantage point that conventional social fiction shared with social science reportage, because
he did not wish to make Bigger a brutish object lesson for environ-
mentalism. Still, he stopped short of full identification with Bigger,
which would have been possible had he adopted a first person
point of view, because he knew reality to be not only perceptual –
the feelings of fear and hate, elation and confusion that mark
Bigger's progress through the novel – but also objective, in the
sense that it has sources and consequences beyond the reach of
immediate sensory or psychological apprehension.

We have no reason to doubt that, just as Wright said, the sociology of Chicago helped him to know his own story, but when it
came to voicing the story of Bigger Thomas the resources of literature far surpassed the contribution of empirical studies. To put the
matter another way, a major consequence of Wright's redrafting
the contract of realistic fiction so that representation of Bigger's
consciousness became the central element was the opportunity to
construct the narrative as an evolving contest of stories – some
inchoate, others partially completed before they are set aside or
trumped by another tale, and all of them qualifying and redrawing
the portrait of Bigger Thomas until the novel makes room for
Bigger to speak for himself.

The first apparent version of Bigger's story occurs in descriptions by the presiding narrative voice that establish the character's source of behavior. An excellent example occurs in the generalizing remarks about his personality inserted as explanation of Bigger's anxiety about concealing his hysteria from his friends:

> These were the rhythms of his life: indifference and violence; periods of abstract brooding and periods of intense desire; moments of silence and moments of anger – like water ebbing and flowing from the tug of a far-away, invisible force. Being this way was a need of his as deep as eating. He was like a strange plant blooming in the day and wilting at night; but the sun that made it bloom and the cold darkness that made it wilt were never seen. It was his own sun and darkness, a private and personal sun and darkness (pp. 24–5 [31]).

Standing apart from the world of Bigger while translating his inner experience into the language of third-person fiction, the narrative voice in this passage presents Bigger as the object of environment. Through imagery likening Bigger's psychology, produced amidst the constructions of human society, to the primary forces of gravity and the adaptive processes of plant life, this summary statement conceives Bigger under the dehumanized aspect of naturalism. Although "he is bitterly proud of his swiftly changing moods and boasted when he had to suffer the results of them," Bigger is so thoroughly mystified by his own psyche that no motive is sufficient to spawn premeditated decisive action, no action gratifying enough to be freely justified.

The counterpoint to the descriptions establishing Bigger as the alienated man appears in the versions of his story developed by the institutional agents of white society about his role in the murder of Mary Dalton. Britten, interrogating the Daltons' servant Peggy, seeks to portray him as the pawn of a Jewish Communist conspiracy (pp. 162–3 [179–81]); newspaper accounts of the crime and manhunt portray Bigger as the beast of racist mythology (pp. 206–7 [228–9]); the inquest and visit to the scene of the crime evoke the stereotypes of white womanhood and civilization beleaguered by the dangers of black lust and the anarchic impulses of political radicalism, creating a melodramatic vignette of Bigger as an evil monster who has escaped the control that right-thinking people know must be maintained over the likes of him (pp. 265–86

[289–312]); and finally, Buckley's presentation at the trial combines all of these drafts of white stories into a case endorsed by the state as the definitive narrative about Bigger (pp. 313–22 [342–52]).

Without the murder of Mary, Bigger never would have required an explanatory narrative from white society. The story had already been told countless times in racist discourse. Even after the murder all that remained to do was insert his name and some contemporary detail into a pre-existing narrative. Yet these accounts of Bigger's criminality, by voices that Wright sets across the gulf of race, are not entirely devoid of validity. The scene of the murder does show Bigger physically aroused by Mary, terrified of being discovered in her room, and, in a parody of Othello's killing of Desdemona, impetuously smothering his victim without sense of consequences. Bigger appears similarly driven by irrationality in the grisly scenes of the disposal of the body. Moreover, the racist versions of Bigger's story bear crucial resemblance to the summary statements of his psychology related early in the novel, out of intimate knowledge, by the presiding narrative voice. Both accounts portray him as the unwitting creature of impulses working with the constancy of natural forces, although in the one case they are said to be impulses deriving from his race and in the other implied results of his social circumstances.

Such deliberate congruity between the spontaneous expressions of racism and the expository imagery of the narrative's normative voice illustrates just how close Wright himself came to stereotype in his daring attempt to invade the realm of racial discourse at its most basic level. The discursive rationalizations of black subjugation have shown themselves ingeniously adaptable to changing historical circumstances and differentiated levels of usage. When scriptural justifications of slavery spent their force against the moral appeals of abolitionism, apologists for the "peculiar institution" turned to crude biologism and sanctioned exploitation by invoking the mysterious properties of blood, or inventing a Western civilization blacks could not be expected to join because of the disqualification of their African heritage. The range and detail of exclusionary arguments has been matched by a variety in style of utterance accommodating the needs of diversified audiences, so that while some classes of white people might continue to use the blunt language of racial insult that was common parlance in nineteenth-century popular culture, the education and social position others have achieved lend them speech that reflects the subtleties of intellectuals who have directed their study of history and social theory to modernizing discussion of the black "others."[17] If he were to contradict "assumptions – about race, history, social order – that the reader might hold to be self-evident" and foreground the conflict between the suppositions of racism and an antiracist position of equality according "full subjectivity to the black protagonist and full authority to the black author,"[18] Wright had to produce a shock that would suspend the possibility of readers' immediately marshalling their learned responses. That shock came from Wright's deploying Bigger upon the ground of stereotype and animating his development through violent murders. Wright made his bid to take command of the racial discourse by sweeping away the historical structures of rationalization and the mystifications of language, thereby laying bare the dialectic of the social system and its ideology. Bigger, representative fictive character on the one hand and object of language on the other, is the product of systemic oppression and its embodiment in the patterns of signs and referents that are the currency of American racial discussion. Through a strategy resembling jujitsu, Wright throws the weight of stereotype back upon its source to create a greater shock than the murders – the recognition that those very acts of violence are consequences of the social and linguistic events that created Bigger.

Narrative logic couples this recognition with the empathy created by point of view to open readers to the bitter irony that Bigger's crimes, the actions that seem to deny conclusively his individuality, have a transformative effect. The second book of the novel, "Flight," proceeds to develop the point by description of the catalyzing impact of murder upon Bigger's consciousness. "The thought of what he had done, the awful horror of it" creates "protection between him and a world he feared. He had murdered and had created a new life for himself" (p. 90 [101]). Having literalized the destruction of an offending object that had given shape to his fantasies of retribution, he has taken a step toward freedom. Marked first by recognition that his own family offers an object lesson in the existential bad faith that makes people "blind to what did not fit" their desperate picture of the world, Bigger's new vision accords him also new social insight. Riding on a street-car to the Daltons' house, he reflects that the black people he sees on the snow-covered sidewalks share feelings of fear and shame, making them think of white people as though they were a "great natural force, like a stormy sky looming overhead, or like a deep swirling river stretching suddenly at one's feet in the dark," but unlike the ebbing water and the cyclically blooming and wilting plant previously used to present Bigger's own psychology, the images that arise in his mind now appear to be subject to revision – Bigger envisions collective action of the dispossessed led by a strong ruler in retributive action (pp. 97–8 [108–10]).

In 1940 the startlingly fascist model of social action attributed to Bigger in this passage served the rhetorical effect of cautionary prophecy, a point underlined in *How "Bigger" Was Born*. Today perhaps it can also serve to illustrate further the degree to which the art of *Native Son* can be distinguished from simple realism. The imagery displays the compression of symbolism. Like the brisk characterization of blind Mr. Dalton setting the question of true sight before the reader, the scenes in the furnace room suggesting entry into the horror of Bigger's subconscious and the apparently senseless murders that upon examination turn out to be profound expressions of Bigger's personality, the epiphanies of insight attributed to Bigger shift authority for the narrative from a level of discourse that depends for its verification upon external documentation and verisimilitude to the discourse inherent in the act of making fiction.

The book called "Flight," plotted as a recapitulation of the novel's opening scene of a cornered rat, also reads as an account of Bigger's shedding old ways while undergoing with new vision a forced process of immersion in ghetto life. With false confidence growing out of a failure to comprehend that the exhilaration he feels after murdering Mary is private and ephemeral, Bigger takes the first premeditated action of his life against the white world by concocting alibis, false charges, and a conspiracy to extract ransom from the Daltons. These putative stories are perverse contrivances of signifying. To make his stories genuine instruments of defense and authentic expressions of his life's importance, Bigger must recognize the synthesis of social reality and individual experience that has formed his personality. Intensifying that process by symbolically charging Bigger's flight with the racially connotative imagery of snow falling on the black ghetto sealed off from the rest of the city by police, Wright represents Bigger as instructed by the facts of black life. Wandering in an abandoned building, for example, Bigger looks down into a nearby room containing two small iron beds. "In one bed sat three naked black children looking across the room to the other bed on which lay a man and woman, both naked and black in the sunlight. There were quick, jerky movements on the bed where the man and woman lay, and the three children were watching" (p. 209 [231]). Omitting the authorial simile and metaphor used earlier to describe the state of Bigger's feelings, this passage suggests that Bigger has arrived at a level of consciousness where perception no longer needs the translation of a mediating voice. It is Bigger's own act of perception that infers the quality of life in physical condition. There is a measure of freedom in that, for as Wright had once written, "at the moment when a people begin to realize a *meaning* in their suffering, the civilization that engenders that suffering is doomed."[19]

The meaning Bigger derives from being forced to witness ghetto life with new vision includes both recognition that the circumstances of oppression are artifices resulting from deliberate human actions, no more inevitable than the cycles that govern his moods, and awareness that his idea of utopia may be glimpsed in the moments when he yearns not to be categorically lumped in the mass because of his race but freely "to merge himself with others and be a part of this world, to lose himself in it so he could find himself, to be allowed a chance to live like others, even though he was black" (p. 204 [226]). In his sensing that meaning flows from human will is correction of the split between mind and environment that had made Bigger the victim of emotions he could not control, the repair of alienation. Appropriately Wright symbolizes the possibility of redemption for this "wretched of the earth" by making his captors curse and revile him while pinning him in the snow "as though about to crucify him."

In his new condition Bigger moves into the book of "Fate" prepared to take an active role in inscribing his story in the developing discourse. Under police questioning designed to make him the scapegoat for a number of unsolved crimes — an intention entirely consistent with the discursive habit of assuming that all blacks are the same — he refuses to provide anything more than the bare facts of the crime he did commit. Because describing the crime that he has made the expression of his very being would involve "an explanation of his entire life," he responds listlessly to each question, wondering "how he could link up his bare actions with what he had felt" (pp. 262, 263 [286, 287]). Similarly, he refuses the frames for his story suggested by the tableau in his jail cell where his mother, siblings, the Daltons, and the Reverend Hammond are gathered waiting to translate his deeds into their own codes, into one or another sanctioned narrative that would repress the motives and philosophical consequences of his crime. Only Jan, who detaches himself from the assemblage by a willed effort to understand Bigger, allows him the right to hate, and thus accepts the premise of the autobiography Bigger yearns to voice.

That it is Jan the Communist who becomes the first white person Bigger knows who does not represent a personal threat, and the fact that it is Jan who is apparently responsible for bringing Bigger's criminal case to the attention of the International Labor Defense and the attorney Boris Max, has both political and narrative significance. At the time he was writing *Native Son* Wright was a committed member of the Communist Party of the United States, lending his abilities and energy to the party program that included extensive work on behalf of Negro rights and the party ideology that approached black ethnicity by asserting that Afro-Americans constituted a nation within the nation. So it is not surprising that Jan and Max are valorized in the novel as examples of progressive whites who by reason of their politics are motivated to give Bigger his day in court.

It would not be fair, though, to read either Jan's exemplification of the possibility of white *anti*racism or Max's more extensive role in fighting by proxy for Bigger as simply occasions for the insertion of propaganda required by party discipline. For one thing, in the 1930s and 1940s the Communist Party was exceptional enough in

its support for Negro rights that the appearance of sympathy toward party figures in a novel written by a politically active black
author in 1940 may be no more unusual than, say, the occurrence
of New Deal sentiments in other fiction. Much more important
than political deference is the use Wright makes of Max as an
integral part of the narrative of *Native Son*.

It is an important part of Max's job as defense attorney to inter-
rogate his client, but in the lengthy scene where Wright records
that procedure he exceeds realism to show a therapeutic conversation developing between Max and Bigger.[20] By directive questioning that covers Bigger's experience with American institutions, his
motives, and his past and present feelings, Max provides organization and stimulus for the autobiography, "the explanation of his
entire life," that Bigger has yearned to tell since his life has been
transformed by the murders (pp. 293–304 [320–32]). Despairing
of communication because all previous characters had believed
they knew Bigger's story better than he did, he had resorted to
gestures of rejection. Under Max's influence, though, he recreates
events of the past, relives the critical night of the murder, and
continues the self-examination that is necessary preparation for
articulation of a life story. Significantly he ends the night's reflection with a new will to live, to learn, to make the connections that
would explain his place in history and affirm the integrity of his
life's story.

The second instrumental contribution made by Boris Max to the
articulation of Bigger's accurate story is, of course, the speech of
defense he makes in the courtroom. It may seem perfectly obvious
to say that a defense attorney's speech constitutes the alleged criminal's story, but in fact the system of jurisprudence makes it more
likely that a defense speech will be part of a lawyerly duel over
material and circumstantial evidence, definitions of reasonable
doubt, and legal precedents. The contest of the courtroom requires
professional knowledge ordinarily lacking in the defendant. Not
surprisingly, then, forensic discourse usually constructs a criminal
case in ways quite unlike those the defendant himself might use.
As Wright creates Max's speech, however, he steps away from
legal language to revoice, through the person of Max, principles
previously stated by the presiding narrative voice.[21] Opening the

defense, Max places his remarks, just as the master narrative does, against the background of racially bigoted discourse that has already conditioned the mob to thirst for blood and biased the judge toward a finding of guilt. Focusing on motive, which is the one element of the crime most mysterious to white society, Max recalls the dominant emotions of Bigger's life, including the mistake of taking "a whole race of men as a part of the natural structure of the universe and of his acting toward them accordingly" (p. 333 [363–4]). And evoking the consequences of the crime in Bigger, Max describes the murder precisely in the way we have learned from the account of Bigger's consciousness to view it: as inevitable, yet as an act for which Bigger has accepted responsibility because it has introduced him to the condition of freedom where he can feel that his choices are significant and that his actions carry weight.

The evident revoicing of narrative themes in Max's speech should not obscure its literary novelty. Even as Wright anticipated the possibility that readers might allow the sensational effect of his novel to forestall full understanding and elected to give them a conceptual summary enforced by the dramatic setting of a courtroom, where life is judged and a death sentence passed, it is nonetheless more notable that he chose to do so by a remarkable inversion of realistic reference. Where customarily character and plot receive verification through fidelity to evidence available in expository documents, Max's speech derives its corroboration from the fictional narrative. For when Max posits Bigger as a product of the historical development of America and makes the thoroughly Marxist claim that the court, which is accustomed to deciding issues of justice for the individual on the basis of personal guilt, should disregard such matters in favor of a broader social analysis, we seek confirmation of the statements not in empirical research or testimony appended to the text but rather in the artistic representation of Bigger's life in the novel itself, most particularly in that element of his life that we cannot know in any other way than through fiction – his thoughts and feelings, unknown in the experience of real life.

For readers the immediate instrumental value of Max's speech lies in the map it provides of the novel's reality. However, introduced into the text in a voice distinct from that of the authorial narrator and more deeply implicated in the events of the novel, the speech delivered as direct response to Buckley's also encapsulates Wright's challenge to American discourse on race. Exaggerated though Buckley's speech may appear today in its vicious imagery and tone, in 1940 it was unexceptionable, and in any case even if it were presented in more cautious and acceptable rhetoric it would remain a précis of the beliefs that justify the subordinate status of blacks as the "other." Max's speech, premised on human equality and fraternity, applies the tools of analysis that Wright found so appealing in Marxism to demystify racist arguments and explain them historically. In this respect the speech also parallels Wright's jujitsu treatment of stereotype.

Naturally enough Max's speech does not carry the same import for Bigger that it does for readers. Bigger inspires the speech, and it is a version of his life's story told from the standpoint of his figurative significance, but for the very reason that he is representative of an oppressed group the meaning of Max's words has escaped him. The legacy of alienation that has denied him knowledge of "modes of communication, their symbols and images" (p. 353 [386]) has left him with feelings that "clamored for an answer his mind could not give" (p. 350 [383]). Still, he has a driving impulse to talk, and for Max to be his audience, because it was Max who "had given him the faith that at bottom all men lived as he lived and felt as he felt" (p. 353 [386]). With the appeal of the death sentence lost, the final meeting between Max and Bigger lacks all appearance of a conference between lawyer and client; it is a meeting of two men whom the American racial system has estranged from each other. Bigger pours out his feelings more in monologue than conversation, and Max in equally characteristic fashion replies to Bigger's query about the universality of human needs with a speech illustrating capitalism's interference with the desire to humanize the world for everyone. Then suddenly communication occurs in an unexpected way. Stating his deeply felt conviction that "what I killed for, I *am!* . . . What I killed for must've been good" with a courage that defies his imminent death, Bigger has become the mentor, Max the mute and terrified audience for a declaration of autobiographical essence (pp. 358–9

59

[391–2]). Max's inability to respond and the fact that Bigger's words are left to stand alone without the mediation of authorial commentary serve as the signs that in this novel dedicated to the dramatization of a black man's consciousness the subject has finally found his own unqualified incontrovertible voice.[22]

Bigger's achievement of voice stands as a symbol of the purpose of Afro-American literature. Although Richard Wright had perfectly good reasons for describing *Native Son* as though it embodies an objective truth, the varying accounts of Bigger lacing the novel and the form of Wright's narrative innovations are evidence that his project was meant to engage the patterns of received racial discourse. Exposing some of the traditional views of the "other" as blatant bigotry and rendering other approaches to race inconclusive by undermining confidence in their realism, he raises doubts about even the surety of reason when applied to unfamiliar subjects. No, Wright's intent was not simply to contest truth. Rather it was to secure the right of a black to tell a black story. Just as Bigger Thomas was imprisoned in an environment that provided no words to articulate his alienation, so had the black author been pent up by customs of language that took no account of Afro-American culture and with impunity denied black subjectivity. Marking Bigger's freedom by the power of self-expression, Wright makes Bigger's voice the emblem of his novel signifying that through the brilliant complex of linguistic acts we know as *Native Son* freedom also comes to black writers.

NOTES

1. Ian Watt, *The Rise of the Novel: Studies in Defoe, Richardson and Fielding* (Berkeley: University of California Press, 1957), pp. 31–2.
2. Richard Wright, "Introduction," in St. Clair Drake and Horace R. Cayton, *Black Metropolis: A Study of Negro Life in a Northern City* (New York: Harcourt Brace, 1945; rpt. New York: Harper & Row, 1962), p. xvii.
3. Ibid., pp. xvii–xviii.
4. Ibid., p. xx.
5. For discussion of such corroboration in slave narratives, see Robert B. Stepto, *From Behind the Veil: A Study of Afro-American Narrative*

(Urbana: University of Illinois Press, 1979), pp. 3–31. Stepto also discusses authenticity in relation to Wright's *Black Boy*, pp. 128–62.

6. See the introduction to the present volume.

7. Wright, "Introduction," p. xxvii.

8. A valuable discussion of the odds against the persuasive power of "documentary fiction" appears in Barbara Foley, *Telling the Truth: The Theory and Practice of Documentary Fiction* (Ithaca: Cornell University Press, 1986), p. 265.

9. An excellent study of Bigger's voice contending that it emerges within the novel's internal dialogue rather than from Wright's engagement of extratextual discourse, as this essay argues, appears in James A. Miller's "Bigger Thomas's Quest for Voice and Audience in Richard Wright's *Native Son*," *Callaloo* 9 (1986): 501–6.

10. An accessible discussion of the verbal art of signifying appears in Claudia Mitchell-Kernan, "Signifying," in Alan Dundes, ed., *Mother Wit from the Laughing Barrel* (Englewood Cliffs, N.J.: Prentice-Hall, 1973), pp. 310–28. For treatment of the place of signifying in Afro-American literary tradition, see Henry Louis Gates, "'The Blackness of Blackness': A Critique of the Sign and the Signifying Monkey," in Joe Weixlmann and Chester J. Fontenot, eds., *Studies in Black American Literature* (Greenwood, Fl.: Penkevill, 1984), vol. 1, pp. 129–81.

11. Richard Wright, *Native Son* (New York: Harper, 1940), pp. 167–8 [189]. Subsequent parenthetical references are to this edition, but for the reader's convenience bracketed page references to the Perennial Classic edition will also be provided.

12. All cited reviews may be found in my *Richard Wright: The Critical Reception* (New York: Burt Franklin, 1978). The Book-of-the-Month Club notice appears on pp. 39–40, and the other remarks are by May Cameron, pp. 42–3; Harry Hansen, pp. 47–8; Mary-Carter Roberts, pp. 55–6; the *Time* review appears on pp. 57–8.

13. Reilly, *Critical Reception*, pp. 88–90.

14. Richard Wright, "Rascoe-Baiting," *American Mercury* 50 (July 1940): 376–7.

15. Originally published in *Opportunity* 18 (June 1940), the review is reprinted in Reilly, *Critical Reception*, pp. 95–8.

16. Wright, "Introduction," p. xxx.

17. For a useful historical survey of stereotypes and their expression, see William L. Van Deburg, *Slavery & Race in American Popular Culture* (Madison: University of Wisconsin Press, 1984).

18. The quotations are from the discussion of the Afro-American documentary novel in Foley, *Telling the Truth*, pp. 234–5.

19. Richard Wright, "Blueprint for Negro Writing," *New Challenge* 2 (Fall 1937): 57.

20. In a work published after this essay was drafted Joyce Ann Joyce develops a related argument about Max's agency, indicating that as the novel concludes, the roles of Bigger and Max are reversed, while the dominant narrative virtually disappears. See *Richard Wright's Art of Tragedy* (Iowa City: University of Iowa Press, 1986), pp. 46–9, 69.

21. For interpretation of Max's speech I am indebted to the suggestions of Paul N. Siegel, "The Conclusion of Richard Wright's *Native Son*," *PMLA* 79 (1974): 517–23.

22. For a contrasting interpretation of this scene, namely, that Max is fundamentally incapable of understanding Bigger's humanity, see Joyce, *Wright's Art of Tragedy*, pp. 114–16.

3

Native Sons and Foreign Daughters

TRUDIER HARRIS

T HE black women Richard Wright depicts in *Native Son* (1940) are portrayed as being in league with the oppressors of black men. Wright sets up an opposition in the novel between the native and the foreign, between the American Dream and American ideals in the abstract and Afro-Americans trying to find their place among those ideals, between Bigger as a representative of something larger and freer, indeed more American, than the limitations of the black community and the black women as representatives of a culture and a way of life that would stifle such aspirations. Wright thereby creates a paradoxical position for the black women in the novel. By preaching subservience, especially in the acceptance of and training for menial jobs, the women act in ways that are antithetical or "foreign" to individual black development, but commensurate with or "native" to what whites want for blacks. The women provide a contrast to Bigger, who, in his desire to break out of the confines of racism, adheres to American individualism: in his most idealistic conception, he is "native" to the best of American traditions and "foreign" to Afro-American subservience. While the dichotomy between native and foreign might be oppositional, it is one that serves, from the women's point of view, to support the status quo. One consequence of the women's identification with acceptable patterns of black behavior is that they inadvertently perpetuate the negative values of the larger culture, with whose positive potential for upward mobility Bigger prefers to identify. In other words, Bigger's dreaming is positive while the women's stifling of dreams is negative, but their very desire for him to remain a part of the invisible black masses is in keeping with the notion of place whites have defined for black

63

people, who, from the whites' perspective, should not dream their way into any of the benefits of that larger world. The function of black female character in the novel, therefore, is superficially contradictory but is true to Wright's notion of what black women are and what they believe: they will use the larger world in quiet, unassuming ways in their efforts to carry out their mundane wills in the black community.

Black women's shared responsibility for the plight of the black man takes the shape of insensitivity to Bigger's plight, adoption of the ideals of manhood espoused by the larger culture and the imposition of those values on Bigger, and failure to offer understanding and support of Bigger *as male*. Bigger's mother Mrs. Thomas, his sister Vera, and Bessie, his girlfriend, are women who want desperately to belong to the invisible masses of blacks who get along with whites by holding the pitiful jobs they have, such as washerwomen and domestics, or training for "acceptable" ones, such as seamstresses. Their personalities render them incapable of challenging or even privately questioning the society that has taught them to be satisfied with grubbing around in the racial cages constructed for them.

All of the women desire to be safe from white accusations that they are out of the place prescribed and defined for them. Thus they will always be acquiescent mammies rather than tricksters or potential militants. They will take only small, indirect actions of defiance against the society that dehumanizes them, because they cannot conceive of direct confrontation. Bessie, for example, will allow Bigger and his friends to steal from the whites for whom she works, but the idea that she may be caught sends her into spasms of fear. Like Mrs. Thomas and Vera, she may confront Bigger directly, but she is utterly incapable of extending that confrontation from the black environment to the white one that oppresses both her and Bigger. All the women, therefore, through their desire to be safe, assist in maintaining the very forces that oppress them psychologically, and that oppress black men both physically and psychologically. After all, black women have always had rather free access to the homes of whites through their domestic and child-rearing obligations. They have made their peace as best they could, but the space itself was not prohibited to them. Black men, on the other hand, have found certain spaces off limits; indeed, as Wright points out in *Black Boy* (1945) and Ed Bullins in *The Gentleman Caller* (1969), they have frequently found themselves barred from those spaces by their own black spouses, lovers, and mothers.

The black women in *Native Son* are all content to nag rather than nurture. While that is certainly true of Mrs. Thomas in the role of mother, it is no less true of Vera when she advises Bigger to leave his gang and pursue the higher road of the Dalton job, or of Bessie when she pouts at Bigger's lapses or whines in reaction to his troubles. As a black mother, Mrs. Thomas is a mixture of misdirected strength and unexplained weakness, of practicality and reliance upon God. She makes demands of Bigger in that "loud, colored" way usually associated with emasculating black women who use their God and their religion as a way to keep black men humble and confined to the places assigned to them by the larger society. Mrs. Thomas succeeds in creating a sense of guilt in Bigger – guilt about his inability to function as a man, guilt about his inability to support his family, guilt about what he does with the other boys when she is not physically watching over him.

The pressure of family life, with the mother as presumed head, is one of the motivating factors in Bigger's later behavior. Mrs. Thomas becomes, therefore, a part of the problem, not a respite from it. There is no peace for Bigger at home with a nagging mother, an insecure sister, and an acquiescent brother whose temperament identifies him with the females in the family. Unable to show understanding toward her son or to inspire any change in his behavior, Mrs. Thomas perhaps inadvertently joins his list of accusers. Her inability to see beyond the here and now, except in an otherworldly way – in effect, her inability to dream – puts her on the side of those who would keep Bigger out of the airplanes he wishes to fly. Too busy with practical concerns to think beyond them, Mrs. Thomas, like Ruth Younger in *A Raisin in the Sun* (1959), is viewed as an insensitive black woman who would tie the men in her life to the plodding, pedestrian cares of everyday existence rather than permitting them to fly – either literally or symbolically.

While Bigger dreams of flying airplanes, the women think only of where the next week's rent will come from, of what it would mean to complete a sewing class and get a *good* job. These concerns, understandably practical and certainly acceptable, nonetheless make the women plodders while Bigger soars, although temporarily, to at least a limited height of creativity. It is Bigger upon whom discussions of creativity in Wright's novel have centered. By killing Mary Dalton, Bigger focuses the chaos of his life into an ordered self-conception; through a creative act of violence, he reaches a higher level of consciousness, of self-reflection, than is possible for any of the women. Even the rather childish and unrealistic scene in which Bigger and Gus "play white" exemplifies a degree of creativity, an enlightened vision of the discrepancies of wealth and power in this country, that is never given to the females in the novel. The power of imagination is Bigger's alone; his soaring might lead to his destruction, but he has dared to fly. He grows, despite his defeat, far beyond any of the female characters, all of whom remain locked into the cubbyholes of blindness and fear they have created for themselves in reaction to and with the consent of the larger society.

In her plodding around upon her margin of safety, Mrs. Thomas is a burden to Bigger – as Bessie will be later on. She is a burden in terms of the philosophy she holds – that getting a job will make everything all right – because the circumstances of Bigger's life will not be eased simply by his getting a job. She is also a burden in the sense of the forced responsibility Bigger feels for her (and for his sister and brother) in his role as involuntary head of the household. To illustrate Bigger's acute repression by these circumstances, Wright strips from Mrs. Thomas any sense of the independent resourcefulness that characterized so many of her sisters throughout Afro-American history and literature. Mrs. Thomas is a defeated woman, one who urges her son to take responsibility for a family in which he is son, not husband or father. Implied, but not stated, in her interactions with her son is the notion that she holds him accountable for the absence of other men in her life. Because her husband has been taken from her, Bigger must take his place. Because she has no extended family in the area, Bigger must provide the support that such relatives could have provided. Her expectations for Bigger, Wright implies, are too extreme; she fails to consider the social traps in which Bigger is caught even as she pleads with him to help the family break out of those traps. She is presented, therefore, as being shortsighted – uninformed about or unwilling to see the larger situation in which she and her family are caught.

Mrs. Thomas vacillates between strong-armed, matriarchal, emasculating declarations and something approaching feminine guile. When Bigger waves the dead rat in front of Vera, Mrs. Thomas is bitter in her reprimand: "Bigger, sometimes I wonder why I birthed you."[1] Implicit in the statement is the accusation that Bigger has failed to meet the expectations held out for him as the firstborn son of the family. A mother's expression of such regret must be as warping to a child as the mental and geographical strictures placed on him by whites. Mrs. Thomas continues the assault by asserting that the family "wouldn't have to live" in a "garbage dump" if Bigger had "any manhood" in him (p. 7 [12]). She further claims that it is his lack of manhood that keeps them in an apartment where rats are as regular tenants as they are: "Bigger, honest, you are the most no-countest man I ever seen in all my life!" (p. 8 [12]). Her verbal harangues clash directly with her urging of Bigger to take the relief job. She tries to provoke him into changing his behavior by drawing upon whatever inner spark of respect may be left, a spark that her own actions rather contradictorily have the effect of diminishing. If Bigger were a man, she adamantly asserts, he would fulfill the Western ideal as provider and protector. That he does not fit the pattern becomes a direct negative reflection upon Mrs. Thomas herself. To her mind, her own failure is ever before her in the very creation of a faulty specimen of manhood.

Her harshness, behind which lies desperation and the disappointment characteristic of a mother toward her wayward son, is also rooted in a struggling woman's disappointment in all men. Mrs. Thomas's husband, even if through no fault of his own, has left the family at the mercy of economic and social forces. The only way she can prevent further deterioration in the family's poverty-stricken condition is to control her sons as effectively as she can. Her verbalization of Bigger's "no-countness," something he also feels intensely, may work inversely to protect against further dissolution of the family. Her goal of safety comes before any concern about embarrassing Bigger, which makes her lack of gentleness with his feelings true to the matriarchal traits in her personality, traits even more strongly exhibited in keeping the younger Buddy in line. When he interferes in the conversation in which Mrs. Thomas is encouraging Bigger to take the job offered by the relief agency, she exclaims: "You shut your mouth, Buddy, or get up from this table . . . I'm not going to take any stinking sass from you. One fool in the family's enough" (p. 10 [15]). The voice epitomizes the strong black female controller of her family that Lorraine Hansberry would immortalize several years later in the character of Mama Lena Younger in *A Raisin in the Sun*. That voice owes explanation only to itself and demands that those nearby show the requisite respect; Mrs. Thomas's reaction to Buddy's comment is a striking contrast to her ignoring of Vera's interference in the conversation. Because Vera offers support and Buddy dares to challenge, battle lines are drawn between males and females in the scene, between potential nurturers and homemakers on the one hand and potential violators and street people on the other.

Yet only a breath after her reprimand of Buddy, Mrs. Thomas shows the other extreme in her repertoire of control; she resorts to an almost tender plea that is rendered ineffective only because its motivation is so blatantly obvious: "'If you get that job,' his mother said in a low, kind tone of voice, busy slicing a loaf of bread, 'I can fix up a nice place for you children. You could be comfortable and not have to live like pigs.'" Vera's comment that "Bigger ain't decent enough to think of nothing like that" (p. 10 [15]) again brings no reaction from Mrs. Thomas, because it is her own party line.

In her transition from insult to cajoling, Mrs. Thomas shows the compartmentalization in character typical of the black woman who bows and scrapes in the white world and rules with an iron hand in the black household. But there are other seeming inconsistencies in her character. The part of the scene in which Vera and her mother seek refuge from the rat shows a helplessness traditionally uncharacteristic of black females and of mothers in general. It is also not in keeping with the matriarchal woman who commands one son to be quiet and calls the other a fool: "Frantically, Vera climbed upon the bed and the woman caught hold of her. With their arms entwined about each other, the black mother and the brown daughter gazed open-mouthed at the trunk in the corner" (p. 4 [8]). Again lacking resourcefulness and a will to survive, the women, especially the mother, become victims of their own fear, dependent upon Bigger to rescue them. There is no strong-willed desire on the mother's part to save her daughter, as maternal instinct might otherwise dictate. Wright simply twists natural tendencies in such a way that Mrs. Thomas can blame Bigger, once again, for the family's plight, for their living in a rat-infested tenement. So anxious is Wright, even in small ways, to place blame on black women for Bigger's personality that he is willing to distort natural bonds of affection between mothers and children to achieve that goal. This distorting characterization continues in Mrs. Thomas's crying response once the rat is dead; weak in character and in will, she is more the child than the mother, more the helpless lover than the protecting parent. Her unwillingness to fight for Vera's safety stands in a marked contrast to a later episode in the novel when she is more than willing to plead for Bigger's safety. There is an inherent contradiction between the two actions.

Yet in her pleading to Mr. and Mrs. Dalton to spare Bigger's life in the later scene, she becomes an embarrassment to him. There Wright sets up a clash between high culture and folk culture, between education and illiteracy, and between gentility and rawness. In all of these pairings, the latter qualities are degraded, and Bigger is embarrassed as a result. In other words, Wright suggests in this scene that a large part of Bigger's problem is that he is descended from such an ignorant, praying group of backward "niggers." The crawling plea that Mrs. Thomas makes become an objective correlative of Bigger's own tortured state with whites. He has tried desperately to retain a semblance of dignity, to show that he has not been stripped of everything that distinguishes him as a human being. Then his mother arrives and puts on a minstrel show for the Daltons, showing thereby that Bigger is everything they and Buckley have believed him to be. Mrs. Thomas's thanking of the Daltons for not forcing her to move is another slap at Bigger's dignity, for perhaps he would have preferred seeing his family move to seeing his mother humiliate herself before the people who have made him feel less than a human being: "Bigger's shame for his mother amounted to hate. He stood with clenched fists, his eyes burning. He felt that in another moment he would have leaped at her" (p. 257 [280]).

In her pleading with the Daltons to spare Bigger, Mrs. Thomas plays well the role of the anguished mother, one who has shortly before given her son over to the care of the Lord. In the book, however, religion is a dead-end proposition. The fact that Mrs. Thomas adheres to it amounts to her washing her hands of Bigger. She says as much in her admonition to him: "The Lord knows I did all I could for you and your sister and brother. I scrubbed and washed and ironed from morning till night, day in and day out, as long as I had strength in my old body. I did all I know how, son, and if I left anything undone, it's just 'cause I didn't know. . . . Honey, your poor old ma can't do nothing now. I'm old and this is too much for me. I'm at the end of my rope. . . . We leaving you now with God, Bigger" (pp. 254, 255 [277, 279]). She has maintained in the opening scene, when Vera asserts that she will soon be able to work: "I reckon I'll be dead then. I reckon God'll call me home" (p. 9 [13]). Such self-martyrdom is a pathetic attempt by Mrs. Thomas to absolve herself of any responsibility for how Bigger has turned out.

Mrs. Thomas could, if she were genuinely and realistically concerned about her son, do much more than pray. She could talk with the lawyers or judges, try to influence public opinion, get her minister to take a more active role in Bigger's defense. Instead, Wright again limits her character, sacrificing motherly affection to make a point about the ineffectiveness of religion. He allows Mrs. Thomas to give up her son; by enabling her to transcend her earthly problems, Wright shows the practical failure of religion in this world. Mrs. Thomas is painted as having little conception of the reality of Bigger's plight except as it could possibly affect her seeing him in heaven. All the stages in between are irrelevant to her, if only Bigger will consent to pray.

Mrs. Thomas and Vera become mirrors reflecting back to Bigger his physical and social impotence. He sees such a reflection in all their actions – and even in their lack of action. He can see in his mother's and Vera's very postures the ways in which he has failed to make life easier for them. Vera has in fact adopted her mother's view, seeing Bigger as lacking concern about his family's plight. Inherent in her reaction to him is also the belief that he has fallen short of his responsibilities as a man. Vera maintains that "Bigger ain't decent enough" (p. 10 [15]) to think of taking the relief job so that Mrs. Thomas can fix up the place for them. It is clear that Vera has been socialized into acceptance of her mother's response to the world and that her reactions to her own circumstances will never get her into any trouble. Unlike Bigger and Buddy, Vera is safe. She also echoes her mother's philosophy in her sometimes self-right-eous attitudes toward Bigger. After the breakfast confrontation about the relief job, Vera passes Bigger just outside the apartment building, then turns to admonish him in a miniature version of her mother's mission: "Bigger, please. . . . You're getting a good job now. Why don't you stay away from Jack and Gus and G.H. and keep out of trouble?" (p. 13 [18]). For Vera, as for her mother, trouble with a capital T is something that lurks in wait for those who challenge authority, for those who refuse to rein in their expectations about life and who persist in upsetting the status quo.

Seeing her place clearly, then, Vera defends her mother as repre-sentative of the status quo and perpetuator of safe values. "Don't bite her head off" (p. 10 [14]), she says to Bigger when he is impatient with Mrs. Thomas, and "Ma's talking to you, Bigger" (p. 10 [15]) when he persists in his effort to ignore his mother. The unarticulated virtues Vera is fighting for give her a strength that she does not exhibit anywhere else in the novel (and she has just fainted in fear of the dead rat). Instinct tells her, however, that her fate is to develop the nagging, cajoling role, to spur black men into behavior acceptable to the larger society. She senses that her moth-er's values – if not her current status – are the symbols of survival for black people in America. By contrast, Bigger's trouble-making mode of existence is the path to their destruction.

Her position is made more explicit in the scene in which Bigger announces that he has accepted the job at the Daltons. She croons upon hearing the news: "Goody! Bigger got a job!" and reiterates her transformed view of him a little later: "'Oh, Bigger,' said Vera, tenderly and plaintively" (p. 87 [98]). For the moment, she is the wide-eyed princess celebrating the hero who has charged off into the world to save his family's "kingdom" (though, a few sentences later, she will be angrily fighting with him). In her approval, she lauds Bigger's seeming willingness to accept the ideals that she and her mother hold. She is essentially patting him on the back for being a good boy, one who has stayed out of trouble by doing the right thing. Her encouragement of his action is a polite form of pressure, rendered absurd by the knowledge of Bigger's true situation at the Daltons. She nonetheless becomes in this instance a defender of the faith of subservience. After all, Bigger has become a chauffeur, not the vice-president of a bank.

Vera remains an echo of Mrs. Thomas, too slight in characterization to operate fully within her own space, but developed enough in philosophy to provide support for Mrs. Thomas's position. The Veras and the Mrs. Thomases of the world, Wright suggests, give plausibility to the argument that black women drive black men from their homes and onto the streets. These stereotypical nagging women are capable of judging black men only as dollar signs. If the men acquiesce to their wills, then the women are happy. If the men resist, then the women will cut them to ribbons with their tongues, producing psychological pain from which the men can escape only if they forsake the domestic realm. When Bigger reveals that he has accepted the job at the Daltons, Mrs. Thomas's response is almost absurd in its canned expectations: "'You got a good job, now,' his mother said, 'You ought to work hard and keep it and try to make a man out of yourself. Some day you'll want to get married and have a home of your own. You got your chance now. You always said you never had a chance. Now, you got one'" (p. 87 [97]). Whatever the chauffeur job will offer, it cannot possibly ensure the completeness Mrs. Thomas imagines, though it may — if he is willing to persevere over a period of years, as Green, the chauffeur before him, has done — enable Bigger to improve his economic and educational status. Mrs. Thomas, however, responds to Bigger's job as if that faraway success were a fait accompli, and she applauds Bigger for taking an acceptable path of coexistence with whites.

Vera, Mrs. Thomas, and Bessie are sisters in their collective responses to the white world around them. They prefer not to disturb it, to keep their safe distance if possible, and to wring their hands and cry out to the Lord if that distance is dissolved. Bessie Mears could be thousands of young black women in the cities of the 1930s and 1940s, migrants from the South trapped in unfulfilling jobs from which they can find release only in sex and alcohol. Bessie, like Mrs. Thomas and Vera, is cut off from any of the usual sustaining institutions in black communities, a problem that critics have pointed out in the novel. Although she frequently invokes the name of the Lord, she is not actively involved with any church, and the usual kinds of support groups, such as women's clubs and neighbors, seem to be unavailable to her; in her social and cultural isolation, she is much like Ida Scott in James Baldwin's *Another Country* (1962). Afloat in a world of manipulators and manipulated, she easily falls into the latter category, a willing victim to be molded and shaped by Bigger's whims and desires. She has little social being beyond what Bigger gives her, whether it is a trip to Ernie's Kitchen Shack or to the Paris Grill for a drink. Bessie is painted as living an empty life, one in which there is little excitement and few opportunities for change. She is gullible, timid, and frightened.

Free in her sexual activity, Bessie has no concern for the possibility that she might become pregnant and thereby create even more social and financial difficulty for herself. Her situation contrasts with that of Zora Neale Hurston's Janie, whose lack of concern about and interest in children we can attribute to Hurston's own professional inclination – what was not a concern for the author is not a concern for the character. For Wright, who also writes out of his own experience, Bessie's freedom with her body might go back to a young woman he knew in Memphis, who almost literally threw herself at him. She saw her body as a way of getting him; and if she became pregnant, that would only solidify the commitment Wright or some other young man would be forced into.[2] While Bessie does not seem enlightened enough to be concerned about marriage, she too has no care for saving her "pearl without price." Her actions smack of promiscuity, and Bigger, the predatory animal, is ever ready to take advantage of a woman who mistakes sex for love and the purchase of drinks for caring.

Bessie is worth no more to Bigger than the sum of her bodily parts. In his depiction of their relationship, in his emphasis on "woman as body of woman," Wright anticipates the role of Cross Damon in *The Outsider* (1953); there is little essence beyond the sexual. Bessie demands little more of Bigger than that he be available on a fairly regular basis to satisfy her physical needs.

Bessie prefers existence on a mundane, routine level – going to work, coming home and getting drunk or having sex with Bigger, going to work again. When that routine is interrupted, she has no way to alter her behavior. She likes the money Bigger brings to her after taking it from Mary's purse, but she does not want to face the consequences of how he obtained it. Her preference for not upsetting the status quo is not rooted in religion – as Mrs. Thomas's is – nor in a personal code of ethics that would make it wrong for her to join Bigger in his plot; rather, it is rooted in a basic weakness in character, an all-consuming fear of being distinguished from the masses of blacks and sought out as an offender of whites. She does not wish to take chances, to dream of a better life with Bigger; she prefers her boring routine. In her effort to ensure that routine, she creates religious substitutes that are as consuming for her as Christianity is for Mrs. Thomas.

While Mrs. Thomas is the stereotypical image of the praying black woman who looks for otherworldly assistance, Bessie turns to escapes within this world. Her calling on God comes from habit instead of belief, and there is little evidence that she ever actually prays. What she does is to turn to sex and alcohol, both of which have become forms of religion to her, serving the function of numbing her to her present situation. Since alcohol is more immediately available to her than sex, it is the crutch perhaps more comparable to the religion of Mrs. Thomas. The initial feelings of pleasure derived from drinking can certainly be compared to the ecstatic feelings of transcendence attendant upon religious experiences, especially when shouting is involved. Alcohol produces the euphoric escape that Wright in his Marxist interpretation of black experience has assigned to religion. Mrs. Thomas and Bessie turn to their respective crutches at various points in the book. As she cooks breakfast, Mrs. Thomas sings:

Life is like a mountain railroad
With an engineer that's brave
We must make the run successful
From the cradle to the grave . . .

(p. 9 [14])

which is far removed from dead rats, joblessness, and wayward children. The engineer in the song who has control over the perilous cliffs on his route has no counterpart in Mrs. Thomas's situation, for she is at the mercy of uncontrollable events that range from the seemingly minor inability to keep rats out of her apartment to the major setback of watching her children live and die in poverty. The city is one cliff to her; her children stand perched precariously on another; and the whites who control where she lives are yet another that she cannot maneuver successfully. Ultimately, the song reflects a pathetic helplessness on the part of those who reach beyond this world for solutions to their problems.

That point is no less graphically made when Mrs. Thomas stands washing a short time later, singing: "Lord, I want to be a Christian,/ In my heart, in my heart" (p. 30 [37]). Even as she sings, Bigger enters the apartment to get his gun for the planned robbery of Blum's. She can escape through singing, but her escape has no real bearing upon the world that weighs her down. Her pursuit of religion, Wright suggests, is a fantasy, not a realistic dream.

Bessie's alcohol is no less a stick of support for her. She reaches for it whenever the circumstances of the world become too much for her. When Bigger introduces his ransom scheme and finally cajoles her into joining him, she turns to drinking once the matter has been settled. She had already been drinking at the Paris Grill when he broached the subject, before the crying scene in which she asserts that she is only going along because he wants her to. As he leaves her there in the dark, her assertion that she is "going to get a pint" leads Bigger to conclude that "that was all right; she was feeling as he knew she always felt" (p. 126 [140]). Looking back as he approaches the streetcar, he observes her "still standing in the snow; she had not moved. She'll be all right, he thought. She'll go along" (p. 127 [141]). Confronted with the possibility of acting against her inclination, of being caught in circumstances she

75

is too weak to control, Bessie turns to the one thing that has sustained her when people have consistently failed her: alcohol. With the stimulus of alcohol she can remove herself from the world, forget about her problems, even if she, like Mrs. Thomas, cannot change them. Her tangible alcohol is just as effective as Mrs. Thomas's intangible religion in moving her beyond what exists and, for a short while, into something else. The stupor the alcohol produces, in which she does not think or feel, is as fantastic as the images of heaven to which Mrs. Thomas resorts in times of trouble. Both are temporary forms of purgation, no matter that Mrs. Thomas may be weighed down even more heavily when her singing or praying ceases, or that Bessie may have terrible hangovers after her stupor-inducing bouts of drinking.

At one point in the novel, Wright allows Bigger to compare Mrs. Thomas and Bessie: "What his mother had was Bessie's whiskey, and Bessie's whiskey was his mother's religion" (p. 204 [226]). Both women have developed coping mechanisms that anticipate the kind of comparison James Baldwin makes in "Sonny's Blues" between religion and heroin. For Sonny, whose problems are too acute for him to face without a crutch, the haze of heroin provides the necessary medium for making life bearable. However, it gives him a feeling of control that neither Bessie nor Mrs. Thomas seeks. Both women are looking for effects that dull, that soothe them out of contemplation of their misery instead of giving them a way of confronting it head on. Sonny can play his music, he believes, much better when he is high. Bessie drinks to forget the white households in which she works and Mrs. Thomas sings her religious songs in a similar effort to transport herself beyond the troubles of the world. Whiskey and religion are both forms of acquiescence, both forms of self-denial. Certainly whiskey can be viewed as a stimulant, but all it stimulates in Bessie's case is acceptance of the drudgery of her life. Mrs. Thomas's religion teaches that his world is a vale of tears, a plethora of troubles that one must endure while working in the vineyard of the Lord. If one suffers long enough, that suffering will eventually produce the desired reward – being carried in the arms of Death, after the manner of Sister Caroline in James Weldon Johnson's "Go Down Death: A Funeral Sermon," and deposited upon the loving breast of Jesus, who will rock away the sorrows of the world and grant the long-awaited rest. Both Mrs. Thomas and Bessie are in the world, not of it. While Mrs. Thomas at least has a vague vision of the next world handed down through the folklore of the church, Bessie cannot imagine any place or any time beyond now. Her escapes through whiskey serve only to highlight how pathetically far she is from being able to make any real change in her life, which is set in a pattern of degradation and misery.

For Bessie, sex is second to alcohol in the escape mechanisms available to her. Bigger takes away her questions about how he has obtained the money he brings by seducing her. Judging by the relaxing moments they share together after their encounter, her enjoyment is presumably equal to his. This short release, however, leaves Bessie sober and inspired, perhaps because of the sexual encounter, to ask more questions about the money and the Daltons. Also, sex is the secondary release because it requires a partner, whereas alcohol does not. As long as she has money, Bessie can indulge her drinking, thereby escaping from the futility of her life and from the images of the white world that demands so much from her.

Religion, alcohol, and sex, as they relate to the black women in *Native Son*, are all reactive activities, indicative of the margin of safety and response to the status quo that are characteristic of their personalities. These crutches allow none of the women the creative urges associated with a desire to fly planes or to escape from the ghetto. For Mrs. Thomas, religion is a worn comfort pulled out for each new crisis. It never spurs her to *do* anything; it is only there waiting once something is done and she needs a way to cope with it. She can therefore call upon her God in reaction to Bigger's laziness or drop to her knees in prayer in reaction to his possible execution. She never uses religion – nor, according to Wright, is it something she *could* use – to contemplate the forging of a new life. The same is true with Bessie in relation to alcohol and sex. Bessie gets drunk in reaction to exploitation by her white employers. She also drinks in reaction to Bigger's absences, and when he visits and she cannot soberly face the troubles he brings with him. Although she wants sex with Bigger, that arena also shows her reacting; she responds to his advances rather than initiating her own.

Love, or those emotions designed to pass for it, similarly supports the white power structure in the novel by being used to pattern acceptable behavior. Mrs. Thomas, through her "love" for Bigger, really wants him to be a good little boy and not cause trouble, in the same way that Wright's mother wanted him to be a good little boy and not fight the white boys when he was growing up. Therein lies safety, which the larger world can applaud because it perpetuates the place defined for black boys. And poor Vera can only follow in Mrs. Thomas's footsteps, expressing love only when the actions of the beloved manifest themselves in adherence to the status quo. Bigger becomes a strange creature who cannot be shown love after he trespasses upon white territory and violates the ultimate taboo by killing Mary Dalton. Vera's reaction to him is comparable to that of Lucy in response to Big Boy after he kills the white man in Wright's story "Big Boy Leaves Home": "Lucy gaped at her brother as though she had never seen him before."[3] Though Bessie allows Bigger to steal from the homes where she works, she does so with her own margin of safety. Her affection, or whatever feelings she has for Bigger, inspire her to keep him within bounds because that will keep her safe. She will be the occasional thief, but never the publicly destructive revolutionary.

Those basic character traits in Bessie override the fact that she initially responds somewhat favorably to Bigger's ransom plan, suggesting that they have to be careful and asking how they can get the ten thousand dollars. Her indecisiveness is clearly tied to her desire not to lose Bigger, thereby extending the initial perception of her character as insecure and malleable, whether by a Bigger Thomas or by the whites for whom she works. Bessie wants peace. Though she prefers it by unforced acquiescence, she is apparently accustomed to some physical abuse from Bigger. She does not convey undue surprise when he threatens to slap her for inquiring about what he has done to Mary, and she is not totally convincing in her show of fear when he threatens to kill her if she does not cooperate with him.

In her dealings with Bigger after the murder, Bessie is most clearly presented as the burden Wright implies all black women are to black men. She wants his body, but not his trouble; she wants his money, but not the responsibility that goes along with it.

The ransom plot is not a situation in which the rightness or wrongness of Bigger's actions are the primary concern; instead, it is a situation in which a black man's quest for freedom is pitted against a black woman's seeming – perhaps subconscious – desire for his defeat. Her actions are a conscious drawing back from the historical circumstances Wright had depicted in earlier works, such as "Big Boy Leaves Home," in which the entire black community joins with the black offender in spiriting him away from the avenging whites. Bessie, even before she is aware of everything that has happened, sets out to separate herself from Bigger. She tries to absolve herself of guilt by asserting that if she participates in the ransom plot it is because Bigger "wants" her to.

Once she knows all the details, her understandable whining and crying makes her even more of a burden, even more liable to be killed in Bigger's increasing inability to distinguish between oppressors and oppressed.

> "All my life's been full of hard trouble. If I wasn't hungry, I was sick. And if I wasn't sick, I was in trouble. I ain't never bothered nobody. I just worked hard every day as long as I can remember, till I was tired enough to drop; then I had to get drunk to forget it. I had to get drunk to sleep. That's all I ever did. And now I'm in this. They looking for me and when they catch me they'll kill me. . . . God only knows why I ever let you treat me this way. I wish to God I never seen you. I wish one of us had died before we was born. God knows I do! All you ever caused me was trouble, just plain black trouble" (pp. 194–5 [215]).

Through his characterization of Bessie as a simpering, weepy woman, Wright directs our sympathies so that her death does not evoke the outrage that might be anticipated in reaction to such graphic brutality. He creates a situation in which the horrible murder of Bessie, despicable through it may be, does not strike at our emotional core as does Mary's. First of all, murder the second time around is by that very sequence not as appalling – and we have seen enough of Bigger's character by the time of Bessie's death to believe that he is capable of almost anything. There is a numbing of reader response. The actual fact of Bessie's murder takes second place to Bigger's capacity for atrocity and to Mary's death. Indeed, readers are from one perspective less disturbed by the fact that Bessie is dead than they are calmed by the fact that her whining has ceased. Bessie's death, then, becomes another rape – this time by the author who created her. Instead of visceral human sympathy, Wright evokes an objective, distanced, intellectual reaction to her demise. She becomes the final, emphatic point in his argument about what the system has done to Bigger. In the early scenes, Wright has presented Bessie with all her embarrassing blemishes. He extends that public exposure in the courtroom scene, where even her remains are "raped" by the hungry eyes of the spectators, eagerly and vicariously reliving the scenes of her physical rape and murder. In this instance, Buckley leads the mob in "lynching" her in this voyeuristic way as assuredly as he lynches Bigger in a legal way.

Wright is so intent upon presenting his theme of Bigger being hemmed in by the black women in the novel that he fails to develop the potential he has almost unwittingly created in Bessie. Although he waits until Book Three to put forth his ideas of the Communist influence upon Bigger's life, Bessie has existed as an example of the proletariat throughout. She is representative of the oppressed working classes, the ones who, unlike Mrs. Thomas washing the whites' laundry in her own home, must go out every day and confront exploitation. Wright himself was perhaps so blinded by the treatment of males, particularly in relation to Communist ideology, that he failed to see that Bessie could carry out his theme just as effectively. In her comments to Bigger about her life, she makes a necessary step in the direction of self-revelation, but Wright stifles that potential by refocusing attention on Bigger and how Bessie is a burden to him. He will not allow Bessie's plight to develop to its full dramatic potential. She remains a fairly one-dimensional character whose brutal murder with a brick – which, as an extension of Communist proletarian symbolism, could suggest black and white skilled laborers building or working together – brings to ironic reversal an image central to the party's propaganda.

Ultimately, Bessie is victimized by everyone, including Wright, Bigger, Buddy, her employers, Buckley, and the reader. Wright does not respect his own creation enough to allow her to live up to her potential; Bigger and the whites for whom she works use

80

Bessie to their own physical and emotional ends; Buckley negates her very humanity; Buddy maintains that because Bigger has a "good job" he can "get a better gal than Bessie" (p. 89 [100]); and readers are forced to dismiss Bessie as their attention is calculatedly focused on Bigger, Mary, and other white characters.

Obviously Bessie did not carry enough value for Wright to be entrusted with putting forth the central point of his novel. In fact, the value he generally places on black women and their world is initially significant by its absence, and then by a degrading comparison to white women. Like many other black writers, Wright uses the movies and the images of whites presented in them as a contrast to the struggling blacks and their everyday problems. *The Gay Woman,* the movie that Bigger and Jack attend while they are waiting to rob Blum's, is a typical example. The "cocktail drinking, dancing, golfing, swimming" world is light-years away from the rat-infested tenement. None of the black women in the novel will ever be a gay woman, will ever have the wealth, position, or leisure shown in that film. Even the gay woman's problems occur at a more sophisticated social and political level than could ever be the case with any of the black women in the novel. Those silver screen images, together with Mary Dalton, point out to Bigger how grossly lacking are the women he knows intimately. The clash of cultures intensifies the devaluing of the black women (and the movies' exaggeration of white reality serves merely to increase the devaluation of black women). In his encounters with black women, in his knowledge of their lives, and in his contrasting experiences with Mary Dalton, Bigger knows that black women are the lowest of the low. It is clear to him nobody cares about them, not even him. Because they do not inspire elevation to pedestals, they can never evoke the respect or distanced admiration that white women can. Bigger can wave a dead rat in Vera's face until she faints, but he becomes tongue-tied and withdrawn in the presence of Mary Dalton. Without even the possibility of being fairy princesses – in the sense of having care, concern, and protection shown them – black women can only occupy present, practical consciousness, not imagination. Bigger could perhaps be inspired to dream about Mary Dalton; Bessie would probably be wrapped in the smells of onion and cabbage, sending any possibility of a dream, as Gwendolyn Brooks suggests in "Kitchenette Building," scurrying down corridors and out the door. In effect, Bigger makes Bessie invisible, from the time in Ernie's Kitchen Shack when he ignores her to the moment when he bashes in her head with a brick. She is to him what he is to the Daltons: someone who cannot be seen because she lacks value for him except as a kind of servant.

The value he places upon them, therefore, does not encourage Wright to lift black women from the realms of archetype and stereotype, to treat them as complex individuals. Mrs. Thomas is ever the mother figure, no matter how problematic that image may become. Bessie will remain a whore, no matter how sympathetic the reader may be to her plight. Little Vera will forever follow in the path of the domestic, eager to learn and use a skill that will keep her invisible.

Wright's manipulation of his black women characters for political purposes ultimately makes them act antithetically to their natural and social impulses. If not so negatively manipulated by Wright, Bessie would perhaps seek out other domestics or working women her age. If Wright were not so intent upon showing the ineffectiveness of religion, Mrs. Thomas could perhaps see that she needs to do more than pray, more than simply leave her son in the hands of racists for whom the cross of the Ku Klux Klan and the cross of Jesus are indistinguishable. If he were not so intent upon showing how pathetic black women can be, Wright would perhaps not allow Mrs. Thomas to pray to Mrs. Dalton as if she were the divinity. In forcing them to follow such paths, Wright limits his black female characters, judging them by a yardstick he does not apply to Bigger.

Bigger's desire to assimilate some of the values of the larger group makes him the native, while the women in their willingness to retain outsider status remain the "foreigners"; they will use what little skills they have to sacrifice their long-term future for short-term practicality, exhibiting a kind of Booker T. Washington mentality. The consequence of such behavior is that they become expendable to Wright — their plights become melodrama, their lives inconsequential. Wright indicts their lifestyles, their values, and, by implication, their very beings. Both the space he gives to them and the spaces he puts them in support this assertion.

Women seem to dominate the claustrophobic interiors of *Native Son,* while males inhabit the open spaces. Although the entire family is cramped in its one-room apartment, Bigger is made to feel that the space belongs more to his mother and his sister than to him. They cook and wash there; he merely sleeps there. They share bonds of domesticity that push him outward to the streets. If the stories we hear of Bessie are true – though she does not seem to verify them – then she would like to trap Bigger into the space represented by her room, into marriage and the very domesticity he tries to escape at the Thomas apartment. In public spaces such as Doc's pool parlor and the theater, Bigger is more at home, though he is afraid when he enters the Dalton yard and home. The things that matter to the women – good jobs, livable surroundings – center upon their cramped spaces, while the pursuit of individual goals that Bigger espouses is much more expansive and open-ended.

In his setting up of oppositions in the novel, Wright's assignment of action to Bigger Thomas and reaction to the women indicates another value-based preference. Bigger's killing of Mary Dalton results from a kind of outrage with the white world. That active kind of emotion is not something that black women in the novel are allowed to express. The feelings that lead Bigger to murder lead the women to religion, sex, and alcohol. Certainly murder would not be a logical response for them, but their lack of creative activity again suggests that they have made peace with the society in ways finally as objectionable to Wright as Bigger's killings are.

In presenting the operative dynamic between Bigger Thomas and the black women in *Native Son,* Wright finally sets up a dichotomy between individuality and conformity. Moving beyond the pattern carved out for him by the larger society, Bigger exhibits a break from convention that, in its healthier manifestations, could be compared to the likes of Huckleberry Finn. In the American system of values, applause is usually extended to the individual who goes against the grain; but such a scheme was never conceived with black individuals in mind. As a group, they have been admonished to conform, to adhere to the status quo if they desired to live, and to suffer the consequences – even to lynching and other violent deaths – if they did not. The black women in *Native Son* can see only the margin of safety inherent in conformity, not its obvious fallacy: that black men are susceptible to death whether or not they conform to the larger society's wishes. Bigger is indeed American and native, then, in his expression of individuality, but the paradox is that the structure was never intended to include him. The women, in their efforts to perpetuate native expectations, ultimately act in manners foreign to the creative, healthy survival of their own black community.

NOTES

1. Richard Wright, *Native Son* (New York: Harper, 1940), p. 7 [11]. Subsequent parenthetical references are to this edition; for the reader's convenience bracketed page references to the Perennial Classic edition will also be provided.
2. Richard Wright, *Black Boy* (New York: Harper, 1945), pp. 182–198.
3. Richard Wright, *Uncle Tom's Children: Four Novellas* (New York: Harper, 1938), p. 34.

4

Richard Wright and the Dynamics of Place in Afro-American Literature

HOUSTON A. BAKER, JR.

1

ONE way to begin an inquiry into the dynamics of Afro-American place is to survey standard inscriptions of place in classic Afro-American literary texts. Ralph Ellison's *Invisible Man* and Richard Wright's *Native Son* provide such texts.[1] In the former, we encounter a scene in which the protagonist, still a neophyte in the Brotherhood movement, and his colleague Tod Clifton are forced into a fight with the nationalist Ras the Exhorter. Ras gets the best of Clifton and raises a knife to slash the boy's throat when suddenly he is overcome by a sobbing surge of feeling. Releasing Clifton, he proceeds to deliver a hortatory condemnation of the Brotherhood and its black membership. His harsh condemnation is matched in its effect only by the eloquence of his invitation to Clifton to join the black nationalists:

> "You [Clifton are] young, don't play you'self cheap, mahn. Don't deny you'self! It took a billion gallons of black blood to make you. Recognize you'self inside and you wan the kings among men . . . You black and beautiful. . . . So why don't you recognize your black duty, mahn, and come jine us?"
>
> His chest was heaving and a note of pleading had come into the harsh voice. He was an exhorter, all right, and I [the protagonist] was caught in the crude, insane eloquence of his plea. He stood there, awaiting an answer. And suddenly a big transport plane came low over the buildings and I looked up to see the firing of its engine, and we were all three silent, watching.
>
> Suddenly the Exhorter shook his fist toward the plane and yelled, "Hell with him, some day we have them too! Hell with him!" (pp. 364–5)

85

This scene powerfully revises the moment in Richard Wright's *Native Son* when Bigger and his friend Gus meet on a South Side Chicago street. While they are leaning against a building, comforting themselves in a sunshine warmer than their kitchenette apartments, their attention is suddenly drawn upward. An acrobatic skywriting plane is spelling out the bold commercial message: USE SPEED GASOLINE. Bigger gazes in childlike wonder and says: "Looks like a little bird" (p. 14 [19]). Gus responds: "Them white boys sure can fly." Bigger continues: "I *could* fly a plane if I had a chance." Gus promptly replies: "If you wasn't black and if you had some money and if they'd let you go to that aviation school, you *could* fly a plane" (p. 14 [20]).

The appearance of the plane in both *Invisible Man* and *Native Son* signifies what might be called a traditional dynamics of Afro-American place. The transport and the skywriter suggest the narrow confinement of black life; they point to a dreadful dichotomy between black and white experience in the New World.

Airplanes and their soaring capabilities are, in one reading of the scenes, signifiers of American industrial/technological arrangements that make traditional Afro-American geographies into a placeless place. Why "placeless"? Because Ras's Harlem, like Bigger's South Side, lacks the quality of place as traditionally defined. The scholar Yi-Fu Tuan gives an idea of the common definition when he insists that the quality of place is a function of space and value:

> In experience the meaning of space often merges with that of place. "Space" is more abstract than "place." What begins as undifferentiated space becomes place as we get to know it better and endow it with value. Architects talk about the spatial qualities of place; they can equally well speak of the locational (place) qualities of space. The ideas "space" and "place" require each other for definition. From the security and stability of place we are aware of the openness, freedom, and threat of space, and vice versa.[2]

Defining space as the possibility of motion, Tuan insists that place is a pause invested with value. From the limitlessness and uncertainty of unexplored space, we win pauses that familiarize space because we invest them with value. MOTHER, for example, may be deemed a valued place within the uncertain spaces of childhood. Essential to Tuan's formulation is a valuing human agency. For place to be recognized as actually PLACE, as a personally valued locale, one must set and maintain the boundaries. If one is constituted and maintained, however, by and within boundaries set by another, then one is not a setter of place but a prisoner of another's desire. Under such conditions what one calls and, perhaps, feels is one's own place would be, from the perspective of human agency, *placeless*. Bereft of determinative control of boundaries, the inhabitant would not be secure in his or her own space but maximally secured by another. Such confinement is always a function of interlocking institutional arrangements.

What the airplanes of *Invisible Man* and *Native Son* reinforce and make further manifest are messages implicit in signs that have already confronted Ellison's and Wright's protagonists. The invisible man, for example, has found himself from the outset of his odyssey encircled by whites who give every sign of their social and technological power. Not only is Ellison's antihero shocked by the actual electricity of white invention, but also by the stinging, crackling challenge thrown at him by white men when he inadvertently utters the phrase "social equality." Indeed, the essential sign is in place when his dream after the first battle royal brings the mocking return of that which the invisible man tries always to repress. The fundamentals of white intention lie in the letter that he finds at the end of a series of boxes, called by his grandfather "years." This primary letter in the protagonist's dream reads: "KEEP THIS NIGGER-BOY RUNNING."

If Bigger needs signs of his confinement other than the cramped, rat-infested quarters to which he shiveringly awakens, he surely receives one prior to his sighting of the plane. He watches workmen mount a looming portrait of the incumbent State's Attorney Buckley. The poster is a parodic sign invented for black territories. Its broad countenance and pointing finger do not say: Uncle Sam Wants You! Instead it reads: IF YOU BREAK THE LAW, YOU CAN'T WIN! Bigger understands that it is *bucks* from the tenement owners that keep the State's Attorney BUCKLEY. He thinks: "You crook. . . . You let whoever pays *you* off win!" The contract between owners and intrusive legal countenances is signed some pages later when Bigger gazes at a South Side board that reads: THIS PROPERTY IS MAN-

AGED BY THE SOUTH SIDE REAL ESTATE COMPANY. The sign prompts the following reflection:

> He had heard that Mr. Dalton [Bigger's employer and the man whose daughter Bigger has murdered] owned the South Side Real Estate Company, and the South Side Real Estate Company owned the house in which he lived. He paid eight dollars a week for one rat-infested room. He had never seen Mr. Dalton until he had come to work for him; his mother always took the rent to the real estate office. Mr. Dalton was somewhere far away, high up, distant, like a god. He owned property all over the Black Belt, and he owned property where white folks lived, too. But Bigger could not live in a building across the "line" (p. 148 [164]).

A corner of the city tumbling down in rot, a territory overseen by Buckley's law, a filthy cell across the "line" above which Mr. Dalton, the owner, soars like a distant god, or a sleek skywriter – this is Bigger's assigned place.

Given the signs, there is just reason for Bigger to want to fly, and there is little wonder that Ras prophesies machines for Harlem: "Hell with him, some day we have them too!" For, in effect, machines connote the abilities of their owners, their pilots and lawgivers, to control all boundaries and invest even what seem to be black localities with a radical instability: KEEP THIS NIGGER-BOY RUNNING.

2

The first cause and longer history that comprise the genesis of such arrangements are not unknown to either Wright or Ellison. It is Wright, though, who most cogently captures this history in locational terms – in terms of place. His depiction occurs in *12 Million Black Voices: A Folk History of the Negro in the United States* (1941). Published the year after *Native Son* had created an enormous impact and catapulted Wright to the forefront of literary celebrity, *12 Million Black Voices* was created in collaboration with the photographer Edwin Rosskam. It stands as one of Wright's most intriguing creations.

12 Million Black Voices adopts for its narration a polyphony of sounds, voices, and tones that have as their source an Afro-American vernacular "us" or "we." There is an intensity of narrative identification in *12 Million Black Voices* that testifies better than some of his fictions to Wright's engagement with the folk. And at the outset of his history, he characterizes the enabling conditions of Afro-American PLACE in their unimaginable violence, terror, and materialism, as well as in their dialectically empowering status in relationship to Western progress.

Michel Fabre, one of Wright's best critics, notes that for Wright the folk history of the Negro was "emblematic of that of the Third World *and of modern man at large.*"[3] The character of this emblematic history is captured by the title of the first section of *12 Million Black Voices* – "Our Strange Birth." The section begins by addressing a "you" who do not "know us." *Your* absence of knowledge results from the fact that "our" outward guise, contoured by 300 years of unremitting oppression, offers a reassuringly familiar look. Beneath this guise, however, lies what the narrator describes as an "uneasily tied knot of pain and hope whose snarled strands converge from many points of time and space."[4] Out of time and space, there converges a knotted (perhaps not-ed, or negated) coil and PLACE that is marked as Afro-American. Its beginning geographies cannot be defined in indigenous African terms, though; they must, instead, be read and inferred – foregrounded, as it were – from the commercial transcriptions of a European commerce that denied, precisely, an African personality:

> We millions of black folk who live in this land were born into Western civilization of a weird and paradoxical birth. The lean, tall, blond men of England, Holland, and Denmark, the dark, short, nervous men of France, Spain, and Portugal, men whose blue and gray and brown eyes glinted with the light of the future, denied our human personalities, tore us from our native soil, weighted our legs with chains, stacked us like cord-wood in the foul holes of clipper ships, dragged us across thousands of miles of ocean, and hurled us into another land, strange and hostile, where for a second time we felt the slow, painful process of a new birth amid conditions harsh and raw (p. 12).

I shall return shortly to the notion of a "second" birth. For the moment, it is sufficient to note that for Wright's narrator an Afro-American semantics of PLACE crushes together two competing definitions of "confine." Definitions of the term as immobility while giving birth and as imprisonment converge in the *hole*, that place of knotted pain and scant hope that is the first, imprisoning birthplace of the Afro-American. The question of generative space bounded into sui generis Afro-American PLACE is answered by *12 Million Black Voices* in the following way:

> Laid out spoon-fashion on the narrow decks of sailing ships, we were transported to this New World so closely packed that the back of the head of one of us nestled between the legs of another. Sometimes 720 of us were jammed into a space 20 feet wide, 120 feet long, and 5 feet high. Week after week we would lie there, tortured and gasping, as the ship heaved and tossed over the waves. In the summer, down in the suffocating depths of those ships, on an eight- or ten-week voyage, we would go crazed for lack of air and water, and in the morning the crew of the ship would discover many of us dead, clutching in rigor mortis at the throats of our friends, wives, or children (p. 14).

When the space of Wright's quoted dimensions is measured out, one realizes there would have been darkness abounding and fever-pitch of noise, crushing weight of compressed bodies rolling in unimaginable stench, a blackout of all signs of a human world, an existence narrowed to the sensations of all that was left – the body in pain.[5] The boundaries set for Africans left them – as Ralph Ellison and Richard Wright suggest in *Invisible Man* and "The Man Who Lived Underground" respectively – *in the hole*.

The British abolitionist Thomas Clarkson, in his account of the nineteenth-century slave trade from Bristol, reported that "the space allotted to each slave on the Atlantic crossing measured five and a half feet in length by sixteen inches in breadth . . . chained two by two, right leg and left leg, right hand and left hand, each slave had less room than a man in a coffin."[6] In Clarkson's testimony, as in *12 Million Black Voices,* we find a conflation. A "strange" Afro-American birth implicitly converges with African death in the fetid hole ("less room than a man in a coffin"). The hole thus stands as an ironic indictment of the commercial birth of modern man.

One might say that the hole, as the PLACE of Afro-American beginnings, is a function *not* of an absence of humanity, a declension of mercy, a racialistic withdrawal of love, but of "trade" pure and simple. The scholar Eric Williams insists that slave trading was distinguishable from other forms of British commerce in a single respect only: its principal commodity was human beings.

PLACE as an Afro-American portion of the world begins in a European DISPLACEMENT of bodies for commercial purposes. Commodification of human beings meant that relationships of property, not free, human, personal relations, marked the spaces between Europeans and Africans. *Ownership* was the watchword over the hole. And within its suffocating spaces occurred a brutal purgation, a violent acclimatization and reaction formation that left a black vessel to be filled.

I have promised to return to the "second birth" mentioned earlier. This second birth is the generational moment that marks the closure of the hole experience, of the first floating instability and suffocation below deck. The narrator of *12 Million Black Voices* makes clear that at the end of a first displacing voyage there was yet another "slow, painful process of a new birth amid conditions harsh and raw" (p. 12). Afro-America was a PLACE *assigned* rather than discovered. The "second" birth was but another deep hole of temporary placelessness from which one had to extract empowering reasons to endure until the next sunrise.

The nature of American plantation agriculture brought the life of this "second" generation into accord with that of their African predecessors with respect to PLACE. The hole was a "place in motion,"[7] a floating signifier of commodified labor. Similarly, the millions bound in Afro-American slavery for the sake of agricultural capital became a floating, ceaselessly moving body of predominantly male, commodified labor. Eric Williams writes:

> The slave planter, in the picturesque nomenclature of the South, is a "land-killer." This serious defect of slavery can be counter-balanced and postponed for a time if fertile soil is practically unlimited. Expansion is a necessity of slave societies; the slave power requires ever fresh conquests.[8]

And following and providing the force for such "conquests" in the plantation South was the great majority of the black population of America. The displacement of the slave trade that produced a placeless — because marked and overseen by others — hole was complemented by a southern agriculture that moved, prodded, drove "gangs" of men ceaselessly south and west, away from exhausted land whose value was defined by Thomas Jefferson when he wrote: "we can buy an acre of new land cheaper than we can manure an old one."⁹ What, then, could be the meaning of Afro-American PLACE within the whole of plantation slave agriculture?

The semantics of place as depicted in *12 Million Black Voices* are captured in a three-fold depiction which we might extrapolate from sections one and two of the book. First, "our bent backs continued to give design and order to the fertile plantations" (p. 24). The place of the black person is that of a tool, of *chattel personal*. Next, "we sit in cabins that have no windowpanes; the floors are made of thin planks of pine. Out in the backyard, over a hole dug in the clay, stands a horizontal slab of oak with an oval opening in it; when it rains, a slow stink drifts over the wet fields" (pp. 57–8). The cabin's space is a function of those bent backs that give design to plantation economies; it is precisely not a proud sign of home ownership. Third, there is the motion in which bent backs and cabins combine:

> Black and white alike . . . go to the pea, celery, orange, grapefruit, cabbage, and lemon crops. Sometimes we walk and sometimes the bosses of the farm factories send their trucks for us. We go from the red land to the brown land, from the brown land to the black land, working our way eastward until we reach the blue Atlantic. . . . We sleep in woods, in barns, in wooden barracks, on sidewalks, and sometimes in jail. Our dog-trot, dog-run, shotgun, and gingerbread shacks fill with ghosts and tumble down from rot" (p. 79).

The motion described is a ritual of "owned" labor — the bent backs moved from place to place with sheltering structures that are only temporary. Like ceremonial huts erected by some preindustrial cultures, the cabin and shack are testimony to motion seen, to rituals enacted for human use, signifying structures momentarily energized by human presence and then abandoned to the elements. They are ghostly, tumbling emblems of ceaseless motion rather than emblems of PLACE. They are signs of the possessed, not of Afro-American possession. Combined with visions of the hole in their past and the urban kitchenette apartments (later described by Wright) as the space to which they give way, it is not difficult to see why the narrator of *12 Million Black Voices* characterizes black PLACE as follows:

> There are millions of us and we are moving in all directions. All of
> our lives we have been catapulted into arenas where, had we
> thought consciously of invading them, we would have hung back.
> A sense of constant change has stolen silently into our lives and has
> become operative in our personalities as a law of living (p. 143).

Displacement and denial of the African personality is compensated
— within the very spaces of the holes of ownership and commodification — by a new operational law of personality. That law is
a law of placeless PLACE, and it transforms a commercial dispossess-
sion into a mirroring alternative to Western economic arrangements.

What emerges from the confined, imprisoning hole is an instability that gives rise to a distinctive folk culture. It is a culture
whose very labor in motion and sui generis conceptualization of
PLACE transform "confinement" into new birth. *12 Million Black
Voices* chronicles this generation as the welding of "a separate unity
with common characteristics of our own" (p. 41). The subtitle of
Wright's narrative — "a folk history" — comes to suggest, then, its
subversive place in historiography. For *12 Million Black Voices* is,
finally, a voicing of a collective countermotion to Western material
acquisitiveness and its desire for stable dominion.

Keepers of the historical discipline in the United States such as
U. B. Phillips and Stanley Elkins have traditionally assumed that
what was coextensive with keeping the "nigger" on the run, or in
"his place," was an extrahistorical position for the Afro-American
folk. Wright's voicing of the story of the twelve million, however,
reveals a space within this running, as it were, an area marked by
self-generated folk boundaries where a distinctive pattern of life
was configured:

> We who have followed the plow . . . have developed a secret life
> and language of our own. . . . We stole words from the grudging
> lips of the Lords of the Land . . . And we charged this meager horde
> of stolen sounds with all the emotions and longings we had; we
> proceeded to build our language in inflections of voice, through
> tonal variety, by hurried speech, in honeyed drawls, by rolling our
> eyes, by flourishing our hands, by assigning to common, simple
> words new meanings, meanings which enabled us to speak of revolt
> in the actual presence of the Lords of the Land without their being
> aware! Our secret language extended our understanding of what

93

slavery meant and gave us the freedom to speak to our brothers in captivity; we polished our new words, caressed them, gave them new shape and color, a new order and tempo, until, though they were the words of the Lords of the Land, they became *our* words, *our* language (p. 40).

The process of transmuting the lexicon of ownership into the unique signifiers of one's own enslaved experience is a self-reflexive description because it mirrors Wright's historical wresting of the essential lineaments of an extraordinary history from a bleak hole. The self-consciousness of the narrator about the nature of his historiographical task is suggested shortly before the above quotation, when he writes:

> To paint the picture of how we live on the tobacco, cane, rice, and cotton plantations is to compete with mighty artists: the movies, the radio, the newspapers, the magazines, and even the Church. They have painted one picture: charming, idyllic, romantic; but we live another: full of the fear of the Lords of the Land, bowing and grinning when we meet white faces, toiling from sun to sun, living in unpainted wooden shacks that sit casually and insecurely upon the red clay (p. 35).

The narrator thus sets himself in opposition to what is known to traditional southern history as the "proslavery argument," the one ironically reinforced even by an abolitionist like Harriet Beecher Stowe when she provides a view of Uncle Tom's dwelling as a "small log building, close adjoining to 'the house'" with "a neat garden-patch, where every summer, strawberries, raspberries, and a variety of fruits and vegetables flourished under careful tending."[10] Stowe's earthly garden, like *Gone With the Wind*'s happy portraiture of slavery, hardly seems akin to the one-room history of *12 Million Black Voices*.

What finally emerges from Wright's history, I think, is a PLACE where there exists a "fragile" black family possessed of a kinship system of its own and sustained by institutions (patterns of behavior) that include codes of conduct vis-à-vis whites and standards of love, hope, and value that find objective correlatives in the Afro-American church and in Afro-American sacred and secular song. At the structural center of *12 Million Black Voices*,[11] after Wright has described the emergence of an Afro-American family based not on "property ownership" but on "love, sympathy, pity, and the goading knowledge that we must work together to make a crop" (p. 60), Wright's folk history moves to Sunday and the dressing, preparation, and departure of a "fragile" black family for church. The type font of the narrative shifts to italic as the narrative voice assumes the office of a black preacher, situating at the center of a black folk history a story of rebellion in heaven, hard earthly trials, the redemptive coming of Christ, and a foreshadowing of the Day of Judgment. The photographs illustrating this section are of collective Afro-American assembly, rapt attention, prayerful enthrallment, and shouted ecstasy.

Returning to roman type, the narrative reads: "The preacher begins to punctuate his words with sharp rhythms, and we are lifted far beyond the boundaries of our daily lives, upward and outward, until, drunk with our enchanted vision, our senses lifted to the burning skies, we do not know who we are, what we are, or where we are . . ." (p. 73). A black folk collective in church takes flight; its consciousness is raised to human heights of genuine "personality." In the third section of *12 Million Black Voices*, the narrator – describing Sunday storefront black assemblies in the North – asserts: "Our churches are centers of social and community life, for we have virtually no other mode of communion and we are usually forbidden to worship God in the temples of the Bosses of the Buildings. The church is the door through which we first walked into Western civilization; religion is the form in which America first allowed our personalities to be expressed" (p. 131). The centrality of the black church for *12 Million Black Voices* reinforces an interpretation of Wright's denotation of PLACE as a dynamic spiritual domain crafted in a sui generis language (i.e., Black Vernacular English).

Black, folk PLACE, though, is scarcely an exclusively religious domain, according to *12 Million Black Voices*. For immediately following the worship service at the center of the narrative and preceding the discussion of storefront churches in section three are energetic characterizations of Afro-American secular rhythms.

The roadside juke of blues harmonicas and shaking hips is the salvific place of the South; frenzied ballrooms, blues, and jazz are the inscriptions of secular energies and personal style in the North.

What both the sacred and the secular occasions of sermons, dance, blues, jazz, and generally energetic collectivity imply is suggested by the following reflection:

> Day after day we labor in the gigantic factories and mills of Western civilization, but we have never been allowed to become an organic part of this civilization; we have yet to share its ultimate hopes and expectations. Its incentives and perspectives, which form the core of meaning for so many millions, have yet to lift our personalities to levels of purpose. Instead, after working all day in one civilization, we go home to our Black Belts of the South . . . our naive, casual, verbal, fluid folk life (p. 127).

A sophisticated, formal, literate, stable Western "civilization" remains the bounding agency for "Negro" existence. Within the confines of that existence, however, the human spirit gives birth to a "brittle" (p. 128) collective life which produces expressive alternatives to Western tradition:

> . . . our hunger for expression finds its form in our wild, raw music, in our invention of slang that winds its way all over America. Our adoration of color goes not into murals, but into dress, into green, red, yellow, blue clothes. When we have some money in our pockets on payday, our laughter and songs make the principal streets of our Black Belts – Lenox Avenue, Beale Street, State Street, South Street, Second Street, Auburn Avenue – famous the earth over (p. 129).

It would be erroneous to overemphasize a valued folk PLACE in *12 Million Black Voices*. For even the engaging descriptions of style at the center of the narrative and the fully orchestrated descriptions of collective style in part three cannot forestall our realization that Wright's history is as much an elegy as a discovery. Section three is entitled "Death on the City Pavements," and it concludes as follows:

> The sands of our simple folk lives run out on the cold city pavements. Winter winds blow, and we feel that our time is nearing its end. Our final days are full of apprehension, for our children grapple with the city. We cannot bear to look at them; they struggle against great odds. Our tired eyes turn away as we hear the tumult of battle (p. 136).

Section four, "Men in the Making," begins not with the voice of the "folk," but with the voice of the children of the folk: "We are the children of the black sharecroppers, the first-born of the city tenements" (p. 142). If, as one person has suggested, city tenements honeycombed with kitchenettes are "vertical slaveships,"[12] then out of their hole have come – in a "third birth" – a new Afro-American generation.

The valued coalition for this new generation is not the brittle, fragile, tenuous folk family of black America, but the "disciplined, class-conscious groups" of collective (read: COMMUNIST) social activism. The narrator tells us that the Great Depression of the 1930s found some blacks mired in the old folkways, longing for Africa, or motivated by an "inarticulate . . . naive, peasant anger" which manifested itself in the 1935 Harlem riot. Class-conscious black industrial laborers, however, were "for the first time in our lives [encountering] the full effect of those forces that tended to reshape our folk consciousness, and a few of us stepped forth and accepted within the confines of our personalities the death of our old folk lives, an acceptance of a death that enabled us to cross class and racial lines, a death that made us free" (p. 144). The crucifying death of a folk culture gives birth to Afro-American, Communist Man as sharer in the Western mechanical dream. One thinks of the concluding dream of *Invisible Man*, in which the bridge as emblem of Western technology is humanized and incorporated into humane existence by the dissemination of bloody black male seed upon the waters.[13]

Similarly, the conclusion of *12 Million Black Voices* is not only utopian, but also aggressively masculine. The very title of its final section – *"Men* in the Making" – provides a specific gender coding. The reasons are not far to seek.

The occupations of the two million blacks who migrated from the South to the North between 1890 and 1920 are described by *12 Million Black Voices* as twofold: "In the main, we black folk earn our living in two ways in the northern cities: we work as domestics or as laborers" (p. 117). Here we have the material reason for Wright's gender coding: in the North, the Afro-American world of work splits into "[black women] domestics" and "[black men] laborers." What is the result?

The result is an essentially Afro-American male vision of the world. That vision projects a merger of Afro-American males with progressive forces of Western industrial technology, a merger that, by the very nature of black women's calling and consciousness, excludes them. The effects of industrial labor on black men are described as follows:

> . . . it is in industry that we [black men] encounter experiences that tend to break down the structure of our folk characters and project us toward the vortex of modern urban life. It is when we are handling picks rather than mops, it is when we are swinging hammers rather than brooms, it is when we are pushing levers rather than dust-cloths that we are gripped and influenced by the world-wide forces that shape and mold the life of Western civilization (p. 117).

By contrast: the "orbit of life is narrow [for black women *domestics*] – from their kitchenette to the white folk's kitchen and back home again – they love the church more than do our men, who find a large measure of the expression of their lives in the mills and factories" (p. 131).

While the narrator's characterization is obviously a rendition of Marxian notions of a determinative connection between the relations of production and states of human consciousness, it is also a somewhat ruthless portrayal of Afro-American women. And it foreshadows the almost scandalous characterization that follows, when *12 Million Black Voices* claims: "More than even that of the American Indian, the consciousness of vast sections of our black women lies beyond the boundaries of the modern world, though they live and work in that world daily" (p. 135). I want to suggest that this scandalizing of the name of Afro-American women is a function of a desperately felt necessity for the black male narrative voice to come into "conscious history" (p. 147).

At the close of *12 Million Black Voices*, black men are industrial workers of the world; they are "in the making" because they have become making men. By contrast, black women are sitting in kitchenettes "deserted, with children about their knees." Rather than workers in the public world of Western progress, they are "domestics."

Their situation remains essentially unchanged from their role during the flourishing days of plantation agriculture in the South, when they worked the "Big Houses" (p. 36) as "Mammies" (p.

37). There is this difference, though, according to Wright's folk history: In the South they seemed to fare easier than black men and to have a relationship to the Lords of the Land that gave them stability, enabling them to be the effective heads of black families. "Because of their enforced intimacy with the Lords of the Land, many of our women, after they were too old to work, were allowed to remain in the slave cabins to tend generations of black children . . . through the years they became symbols of motherhood, retaining in their withered bodies the burden of our folk wisdom, reigning as arbiters in our domestic affairs until we men were freed and had moved to cities where cash-paying jobs enabled us to become the heads of our own families" (p. 37).

What is juxtaposed with the problematic stability of black women implied by this quotation is the phrase "when a gang of us [black men] was sold from one plantation to another" (p. 37). This black male labor in motion contrasts sharply with the black women's static retention of the cabin's space. The interiority of the cabin becomes conflated with the words "intimacy," "motherhood," "folk wisdom," and "domestic," suggesting a different set of markers and boundaries for woman's PLACE in the slave economy.

3

What *12 Million Black Voices* does, in effect, is narrow the geographies of black women in the manner implied by a familiar white southern quip used to justify the exclusion of blacks from educational opportunities: "all the geography a nigger needs to know is how to get from his shack to the plow" (p. 64). The tight rounds of black women's lives seem to run from intimacy, to black childbearing, to domestic servitude in endless white kitchens. The narrator invests such women – in their dotage – with a mystifying folk wisdom, but there is little doubt that the strongest accents of black women's characterization fall on what might be called their essential inessentiality in the progress of black males. They are, in fact, inessentiality *in potentia*.

The word "until" in the earlier passage describing the southern black woman – "until we men were freed . . ." – marks a moment of radical conflation. It renders "her" as the always already displaced. Early on in *12 Million Black Voices*, it summons a future in which black *men* will enter conscious history.

Certainly the goal of close analysis of Wright's delineation of black women is not simply to bring him shamefully before the bar of feminist opinion. *12 Million Black Voices* has its moments of exoneration or, better, amelioration. To cite but one instance, there is the resonant poetry of childbirth:

> Our black children are born to us in our one-room shacks, before crackling log fires, with rusty scissors boiling in tin pans, with black plantation midwives hovering near, with pine-knot flames casting shadows upon the wooden walls, with the sound of kettles of water singing over the fires in the hearths . . . (p. 62).

How different (even with the cringe that attends the word "rusty") this scene is from the "alienated childbirth" described by Adrienne Rich in *Of Woman Born*. In a scathing portrayal, Rich depicts the Western manner of childbirth as a "medical emergency" dominated by male presence, hospital hierarchicalization, analgesia, intrusive forceps, and a general abandonment of the woman.[14] Further, she suggests that children, out of such alienating beginnings, are, at best, perceived as cursed blessings.

By contrast, *12 Million Black Voices* tells us that "a child is a glad thing in the bleak stretches of the cotton country, and our gold is in the hearts of the people we love, in the veins that carry our blood, upon those faces where we catch furtive glimpses of the shape of our humble souls" (p. 59). Wright's lyricism further extends to a definition of the unique relationship between a black folk woman and her children: "no matter what the world may think of them, that [black] mother always welcomes them back with an irreducibly human feeling that stands above the claims of law or property. Our scale of values differs from that of the world from which we have been excluded; our shame is not its shame, and our love is not its love" (p. 61). In this inscription of motherhood in the precincts of the folk, we seem almost to have a valorized space set by the folk themselves. MOTHER seems a black-determined PLACE.

In section three, however, as we have already seen, the black mother's productions comprise a type of orphan-life, one characterized by abandonment (p. 135). Norms are marked by the father's desertion. The "courts and the morgues," therefore, "become crowded with our lost children" (p. 136).

While valued at one point in Wright's narrative, motherhood is scarcely a secure place of refuge. Actually, the stunning place (conscious history) of black men in the making has no complement among domestic black women. Even the procreative function, which in traditional Western bourgeois mystifications is considered a woman's sacred enterprise, is ultimately discounted by Wright's history as an exercise in abandonment. How black men in the making are, in fact, made and nurtured for entry into industrial class-consciousness, therefore, is never made manifest. For woman remains an ahistorical remnant of folk culture. She is decisively not a productive force of Western modernism. With her storefront ecstasy and limited geography, from kitchenette to kitchen, she represents a backwash of conscious history.

4

But, of course, the negative account of black women in *12 Million Black Voices* is not simply a function of some simplistic assignment of occupational roles. No effective analytical end would be achieved, I think, by setting forth a complementary or corrective historical account depicting and praising the virtues and victories of black professional women such as Mary McLeod Bethune, Charlotte Hawkins Brown, and others, or the trade union initiatives of women such as Connie Smith and Moranda Smith (no relation), or the tales of black women escaping domestic drudgery and entering colleges and industry in increasing numbers with the advent of World War II.

It was not that Wright lacked knowledge of black women's roles in the labor movement or the Communist Party. A voracious reader and ardent autodidact, Wright did not lack knowledge. What he lacked, it seems to me, in the specific terms of a dynamics of Afro-American PLACE, was an immunity to the lure of a peculiarly materialist historiography.

It is fair to say, I think, that the implicit subject of *12 Million Black Voices*, as of all histories, is history itself. The historian of Wright's

history, like all historians, must persistently entertain an awareness of the import of each of his discursive gestures in their relationship to a general domain of discourse called "history." Past
events and ascriptions of causality are not simply *historical,* or past,
but functions of the present relation of their writer to a discourse of
containment, i.e., "history." Wright did not receive a revealed vision of the past, but, rather, consciously constructed a folk past in
harmony with and under the guidance of a particular conception
of history. And insofar as his specific "historical" past is a function
of his own discursive construction, we can claim that he did not
simply miss the continent of black women during an innocent and
objective voyage of discovery. No, in fact, he sighted that continent, then refigured it in accord with his preferred historiographical strategies of scientific socialism. The determinants of *12 Million
Black Voices* are to be found in the important critical essay "Blueprint for Negro Writing," which appeared four years before the
publication of the folk history.[15]

In the section of "Blueprint" entitled "The Problem of Perspective" we find the following assertion: "anyone destitute of a theory
about the meaning, structure and direction of modern society is a
lost victim in a world he cannot understand or control" (p. 341).
While discouraging a facile adoption of "isms," Wright is clear
about the necessity for perspective, defined as a governing theory
of the world's operations:

> Perspective is that part of a poem, novel, or play which a writer
> never puts directly upon paper. It is that *fixed point in intellectual
> space* where a writer stands to view the struggles, hopes, and suffer-
> ings of his people (my emphasis, p. 341).

He continues:

> Of all the problems faced by writers who as a whole have never
> allied themselves with world movements, perspective is the most
> difficult of achievement. At its best, perspective is a pre-conscious
> assumption, something which a writer takes for granted, something
> which he wins through his living (pp. 341–2).

Though the mystifying word "pre-conscious" appears in this description, Wright quickly brackets it with "living," or *experience.*
Hence, perspective seems to be the given equivalent in con-

sciousness of a very specific and even individual relationship to the relations of production — "living." A Marxian problematic seems to carry the day.

That word "pre-conscious" continues, however, to haunt perspective, giving it the ambiguous status of both a state of reflection derived from *individualized* experience and a scientifically derivable *donnée* of the relations of production. First, Wright says that perspective means for the Negro writer a reflective consciousness which recognizes the magnitude of the world's working class and understands the connection between the interests (ironically, given his own dismissal of such women) of a "Negro woman hoeing cotton in the South and the men who loll in swivel chairs in Wall Street and take the fruits of her toil" (p. 342). This definition, though, competes with the one that concludes the essay's section on "Perspective":

> Perspective for Negro writers will come when they have looked and brooded so hard and long upon the harsh lot of their race and compared it with the hopes and struggles of minority peoples everywhere that the cold facts have begun to tell them something (p. 342).

"The Problem of Perspective," it seems to me, represents the METAPLACE of Wright's construction of historical and fictive PLACE. And contrary to the specifications of his own blueprint, this place is not *fixed*. It is a floor, or platform, that vibrates with competing motions of race and class as Wright strives to reconcile the formerly alienated interests of the black masses (or nation) with the (Marxian) aims and ends of the Negro writer.

There is no call for an extant or tangible reality where a blueprint is concerned. It is always an idealistic projection of what will be — a metaplace. Hence, Wright can deem the space of his own intellectual occupancy as the place where competing interests converge. The space of a Marxian socialism which privileges the consciousness and interests of the proletariat — of the working industrial classes — becomes, for Wright, a ground on which a racialistically determined Negro separatism or "nationalism" (a folk history, in fact) will transmute itself through dialectical logic into black working-class consciousness.

The mind that provides the blueprint is, in effect, already in

PLACE. It occupies, as it were, a constructing theory as METAPLACE. Wright explicitly offers himself, then, as the architect of both an Afro-American social and artistic revolution in "Blueprint." He is, implicitly, the writer who has made himself over, who has *placed* himself in terms of his own design.

The rub, of course, is that the design is not an original creation, but, in the way of all hermeneutical spaces, a reading or interpretation. And as with all interpretations, there is an unexplained remainder. While class interests and consciousness are supposed to subsume all before them, they cannot, in fact, entirely account for the persistence of a felt nationalism and the tangible activities of the black domestic woman with the hoe. It is this remainder that keeps things in motion.

For Wright's Marxian situation as a writer and his designation of Marxism as the fitting perspective or metaplace of the Afro-American writer has curious results in *12 Million Black Voices*. Negro nationalism, for example, is *not* transmuted, leaving behind valued relics of a former arrangement of black life. And domestic women are *not* read in terms of the combined comprehension of Negro nationalism and Marxian economics suggested in "Blueprint." Instead, they are in effect murdered; they are left to die on city pavements. They are *remaindered,* as my earlier discussion of kitchenettes implies, in deserted spaces of an outworn history.

Bettina Aptheker writes as follows about the erasure of revolutionary woman effected by a Marxian critique:

First, the majority of industrial workers [the proletariat] have been and are men. Women are concentrated precisely in service, clerical, and sales work [non-revolutionary classes] so that our political subordination is built into even the theoretical concepts of the working class. Second, domestic labor – which occupies a substantial portion of most women's time and energy – is designated as "unproductive" and apparently "nonexploitative." It remains, at least theoretically (if not practically), invisible, within the political economy of capitalism. Third, in Marxist theory, the masses of women almost always derive their class status from the men to whom they are attached . . . Women are continually placed on the periphery of the "real" [revolutionary] drama of history.[16]

Bringing together a number of concerns in the dynamics of Afro-American PLACE at this point, we see that Wright's reliance on

Marxism as a METAPLACE left him in the hole. For his choice of a historiographical "fixed place" forced him to eliminate women from Afro-American "conscious history."

Like his successor, Ralph Ellison, Wright allowed the astonishing technological power of the West, represented by factories and machines, to blind him to the woman's (and by implication, "folk") power of a black nation within.[17] Both Ellison and Wright endorse machines as signs of a redemptive modernism. Both are correct about the redemptive *potential* of machines. Their vision fails, however, when it reads the machine as *the text* itself rather than the holographic displacement, the condensation and distortion, as it were, of a dream of power.

We can return now to Wright's airplane urging the use of speed gasoline or to Ellison's transport high above Harlem disorder. Both can be seen as modern inscriptions of the ship on which a FOLK arrived from Africa. The planes are a return of the repressed content of slavery, requiring an immense act of willed belief to be read as hopeful signs of Afro-American modernism.

This Afro-American male will to believe produces a cognitive dissonance in *12 Million Black Voices*:

> On top of this [erosion and rape of the land by timber interests] there come, with a tread as of doom, more and more of the thundering tractors and cotton-picking machines that more and more render our labor useless. Year by year these machines grow from one odd and curious object to be gaped at to thousands that become so deadly in their impersonal labor that we grow to hate them. They do our work better and faster than we can, driving us from plantation to plantation (p. 79).

A shorthand for this quotation reads: machines, by their very conditions of existence (i.e., profit), put us in the hole. But, in a passage cited earlier, we find the following joyous claim: "in industry," black men encounter "experiences that tend to break down the structure of our folk characters and project us toward the vortex of modern urban life" (p. 117).

I want to suggest that both Wright and Ellison mistook the hole of industrial wage slavery for the matrix of a potentially productive black urban modernism. Both mistake machines for productive (if numbing) interiors — wombs — from which a modern, or certainly

105

a revised and redemptive, Afro-American consciousness will be born. Ellison's invisible man, as a case in point, steps from the numbing shocks of a womblike machine in the factory hospital episode and finds that the last thing to be removed from his body is the "cord which was attached to the stomach node" (p. 238). He is birthed by a machine. Wright similarly translates the PLACE of an emergent, modern, industrial Afro-American man as a machine's interior: "It seems as though we are now living inside of a machine; days and events move with a hard reasoning of their own" (p. 100).

The crucial mistake, of course, is in the reading of the machine as woman. The phallic, flying form of planes clearly indicates that they are not wombs. For what, in fact, are dreams of flying? Freud speaks:

> The close connection of flying with the idea of birds explains how it is that in men flying dreams usually have a grossly sensual meaning; and we shall not be surprised when we hear that some dreamer or other is very proud of his powers of flight.[18]

The real consequences of Wright's and Ellison's case of mistaken identity reveal themselves at the conclusions of *Native Son* and *Invisible Man*. The protagonists of both novels are in states of confinement, and neither, I believe, is coming out. Why? Bigger will be electrocuted; preliminary and threatening shocks offered by an array of signs will be translated into his extermination. And the invisible man? Well, he will go on thinking that his extraction of power from Monopolated Light and Power is an act of subversion. In truth, the one thing that the West *always* has in abundance is *power*. What the invisible man may never secure is "responsibility," not as a function of mere power, but as a function of the *control* of power. The end awaiting both protagonists is enough to induce a fear of flying.

5

The fear is justifiable. For sexuality is charged with a complex history within the confines of black folk history. In terms of a dynamics of PLACE, for example, one must note that while slave ships crossing the Atlantic carried black men in their holes, the black women rode elsewhere.

The Afro-American historian Deborah Gray White corrects one traditional view of the slave trade when she writes:

> There was . . . a problem with [Stanley] Elkins' discussion of the Middle Passage [in his study *Slavery*]. Blacks, he insisted, traveled the Atlantic in the holds of slave ships. Elkins was right in his assertion that holds were "packed with suffocating humanity." However, both sexes did not travel the passage the same way. Women made the journey on the quarter and half decks.[19]

White continues:

> Male and female slavery were different from the very beginning. As noted previously, women did not generally travel the middle passage in the holds of slave ships but took the dreaded journey on the quarter deck. According to the 1789 Report of the Committee of the Privy Council, the female passage was further distinguished from that of males in that women and girls were not shackled. The slave trader William Snelgrave mentioned the same policy: "We couple the sturdy Men together with Irons; but we suffer the Women and children to go freely about."[20]

The most descriptive word for general transactions above deck would be "access." "Access" in terms of the African trade translates as "rape" — a violent, terrorizing tactic of abuse sanctioned by ownership and enslavement. If the African men in the coffinlike hole felt the chafing of "iron" and the nauseating roll of the ship's motion as their domination by powerful men who could produce "iron monsters," then African women must have experienced a quite different and unmediated relationship to the slave trader's technology. Theirs could not have been an awestruck response such as that recorded in 1789 by Olaudah Equiano, whose first view of a slaveship riding at anchor on the African coast filled him "with astonishment." When he discovered that the machine moved across the ocean by means of cloth hoisted on its masts, he was further "amazed . . . and really thought they [white men] were spirits."[21]

The hard, physical evidence that the traders were not spirits would have come immediately to African women in the form of rape. Their relationship to white traders was not a sexual one. Instead, it was one of terrorizing power – of phallic horror. As Angela Davis writes in her brilliant essay "The Legacy of Slavery: Standards for a New Womanhood":

> It would be a mistake to regard the institutionalized pattern of rape during slavery as an expression of white men's sexual urges, otherwise stifled by the specter of white womanhood's chastity. Rape was a weapon of domination, a weapon of repression, whose covert goal was to extinguish slave women's will to resist, and in the process, to demoralize their men.[22]

If in the shackled space below deck deep groans betokened the death of mercy and love, then in the open regions of the decks harsh screams signified the brutal demise of inviolate sexuality.

Black women's restriction to plantations while black men were on the move, then, hardly implied "intimacy" in any traditional sense. It was, rather, an extension of white male terror tactics of "access."

We return to Wright's "Blueprint" now with an enlarged historiographical perspective. The ambivalence of Marxian class consciousness and nationalistic concern with race – of "pre-consciousness" and material relations of production – clarifies itself as sexual ambivalence. For if the way of class consciousness implied by a Marxian critique is pursued, then the future will produce an Afro-American modern man, born in mechanical glory from the womb of the machine. If, however, a nationalist history is privileged, black men of the future, like those of the folk past, will continue to be men "of [accessible] woman born."[23]

Asexual birth from the machine displaces a painful history of rape and relegates its victims to an historical void. And valorization of the machine as a sign of the possibilities of a new male proletarian bonding across racial lines necessitates a violent repudiation of the domestic black woman. Ironically, the accessed black woman becomes, out of her very victimization, a hated symbol to be eradicated by aspiring black male consciousness. A Marxian problematic forces the writer to devalue women, therefore, in both folk culture *and* "conscious history." This black male Marxian blind spot, or silence, conditions the fictive texts and tradition of both Wright and Ellison.

If, for example, Bigger Thomas believes the entire world – and especially the white Mrs. Dalton – is blind as a result of its allegiance to an archaic folk and racial perception, Ellison's invisible man is equally contemptuous of those who cannot see. Disguised merely in sunglasses, Ellison's protagonist, like Bigger the murderer, deceives the entire "folk" community.

But surely it is rather Wright and Ellison who have blinded themselves with a kind of transcendentalist optimism, an aggressively male optimism that discounts woman's history (or herstory) in order to project an alliance between black and white male industrial workers as the oversoul of modernism. In America it takes far more than dark glasses, however, to dissolve the old folk category of race. Its inescapable and omnipresent signifier is, in fact, the accessible body of domestic black woman – whether as victim of rape or sufferer of teenage pregnancy. In truth, the only escape from such an indisputable and grounding historical writing of violence is a brutally internecine and intergender violence. What has first to be effected by the black male of Wright's historiography is not transcendence, but murder.

The corollary image of the black man in flight is the image of "black [domestic] woman murdered . . . left to die in the deserted spaces of . . . outworn history." If Bigger's text is skyward, Bessie Mears's story in *Native Son* has clearly to do with death on city pavements. Bessie's story is one that even Ellison, in all his Oedipal subtlety and anxious revisions of Wright, merely repeats.

The prefiguration of the kitchenette women of *12 Million Black Voices* represented by *Native Son's* domestic black woman occurs immediately after Bigger, with money stolen from the murdered body of Mary Dalton, has lured Bessie into sexual intercourse:

> The same deep realization he [Bigger] had had that morning at home at the breakfast table while watching Vera [his sister] and Buddy [his brother] and his mother came back to him; only it was Bessie he was looking at now and seeing how blind she was. He felt the narrow orbit of her life: from her room to the kitchen of the white folks was the farthest she ever moved (p. 118 [131]).

Bessie, however, is scarcely blind. She knows Bigger and the situation of both his and her own life — *intimately*. Here is the dialogue between her and Bigger that takes place a short time later:

> "If you killed *her* [Mary] you'll kill *me*," she said. I ain't in this."
> "Don't be a fool. I love you."
> "You told me you *never* was going to kill."
> "All right. They white folks. They done killed plenty of us" (p. 152 [168]).

To which Bessie responds: "That don't make it right." She is, of course, right — on all counts.

Avatar of the violence of the traders above deck, undeceived about the exploitative intent of their "tools," and victim of a denigrating Western will to domination, Bessie is accessible, domestic, and unprotected. She also possesses the most lucid vision in *Native Son*. She is the *only* character in the novel (and one among the few critics of Bigger Thomas) who realizes that Bigger's murderous course is a mistaken redaction of Western tactics of terror.

Bigger, for example, reflects with calm and cunning self-satisfaction that his relationship to Bessie has been one of commercial trade: "he would give her . . . liquor and she would give him herself. . . . He knew why she liked him; he gave her money for drinks" (p. 118 [132]). As far as Bigger is concerned, it is not black love (or industrial workers' wages) that secures their relationship, but stolen capital. He is a murderer and petty thief who uses Bessie as a means of passage.

The operative word, of course, is "uses," for the entire megalomaniacal scheme of ransom that Bigger concocts relies on Bessie's forced complicity. To gain her compliance, he browbeats, bribes, bullies, and beats her. His greatest anxiety vis-à-vis the black domestic, though, is captured not so much by his early actions as by the phrase he most frequently rehearses: "He could not take her with him and he could not leave her behind" (p. 199 [220]). The suppressed term in this anxious statement is "alive": "he could not leave her behind [alive]." Variously described as a "dangerous burden" (p. 121 [135]) and a weak, accusing, demanding liability (p. 199 [221]), Bessie is coded by *Native Son* in exactly the same terms as the kitchenette domestics of *12 Million Black Voices*. She is the accessible woman who institutes folk history as opposed to conscious modernism. What, then, is to be done with her, or to her, by men in the making? The scene in *Native Son* reads as follows:

> He was rigid; not moving. This was the way it *had* to be. Then he took a deep breath and his hand gripped the brick and shot upward and paused a second and then plunged downward through the darkness to the accompaniment of a deep short grunt from his chest and landed with a thud. *Yes!* (p. 201 [222])

How terrifyingly different *Native Son*'s affirmative is from that of James Joyce's Molly Bloom. For Wright's scene is the murder of Bessie Mears after Bigger has raped her in the deserted spaces of a rotting South Side tenement – a structure which stands as the very emblem of what *12 Million Black Voices* calls "death on the city pavements." Bigger carries her fatally battered body to a window and drops it into an air shaft:

> The body hit and bumped against the narrow sides of the air-shaft as it went down into *blackness*. He heard it strike the bottom (my emphasis, p. 202 [224]).

Significantly, Bigger immediately discovers that he has forgotten to retrieve from Bessie's pocket the remainder of the money stolen from Mary Dalton. Hence, not only the accessible body, but also the currency of accession hits bottom. The old folk order (of "blackness") is dead. Long live the bigger man (of Western culture) in the making!

6

Without a sustaining folk presence, however, as James Baldwin so astutely realized in his critique of Wright's protagonist, Bigger is doomed.[24] He is destined, in fact, not to birth from the machine, but to death in the throes of its numbing power. And it is bitterly appropriate that the raped and murdered body of Bessie Mears should return as witness to Bigger's mistaken interpretations of the skywriter's text. Her body, wheeled into a coroner's inquest, startles Bigger:

> He had completely forgotten Bessie . . . [but] understood what was being done. To offer the dead body of Bessie as evidence and proof

that he had murdered Mary would make him appear a monster; it would stir up more hate against him (p. 281 [306]).

Wright describes his protagonist's additional response as one of sympathy and shame. But the overall import of Bessie's witness is Bigger's indictment.

If Bigger is a product born of mechanistic, Western technology, he is scarcely a maker. He has made nothing: he has forgotten much. His pride in rejecting even a Communist vision of the world as set forth by the ideologue attorney Boris Max — "What I killed for must've been good! . . . I feel all right when I look at it that way" (p. 358 [392]) — should not be conceived in Marxian terms. It must be read, instead, in terms of the Freudian description of flying cited earlier: "in men flying dreams usually have a grossly sensual meaning, and we shall not be surprised when we hear that some dreamer or other is very proud of his powers of flight."

In codifying the dynamics of Afro-American PLACE, it seems necessary, then, to draw a distinction between the locational positions of black men and black women. This necessity is made abundantly clear by Bigger's reflection after Bessie tells him that whites who discover his murder will, surely, accuse him of rape. Bigger reflects:

> Had he raped her [Mary]? Yes, he had raped her . . . But rape was not what one did to women. Rape was what one felt when one's back was against a wall and one had to strike out, whether one wanted to or not, to keep the pack from killing one (pp. 193 [213–214]).

Rape, of course, is *precisely* something done to women. It is not an act of rebellious and heroic black self-defense like Claude McKay's posture in the bellicose poem "If We Must Die." Its signal presence in Afro-American history is a sign of white male domination.

What Wright's historiographical revisionism amounts to, then, is history repeating itself — coming around for a second time like *The Eighteenth Brumaire of Louis Bonaparte* — as parody. Marx begins *The Eighteenth Brumaire* with the observation that Hegel has said that history always repeats itself, comes around again. He forgot to add, said Marx, that the first time it is as tragedy, the second time as farce.[25]

Bigger's murderous actions against Bessie are, finally, second-order redactions of the above-deck violence of white traders and white enslaving machines. Even the language of *Native Son* and *12 Million Black Voices* — with its resonant poems to machines and New World industrial civilization — is parodic in the manner of Louis Bonaparte's guises and rhetorics of the 1789 Revolution *manqué*. The indictment of Wrightian secondary history as farce — the sign of a flawed historiographical vision — is, finally, the brutalized corpse of Bessie Mears.

Bessie's witness in *Native Son*, though, is not merely a parodic corpse. The vision of Wright's domestic is ironically and resonantly expressed in the novel. For though she is denied the status of a laborer in the making, she does, in fact, sing the workingwoman blues in the novel, and the uncanny ambivalence of Wright's METAPLACE reveals its generative force in the novel's actual recording of her blues. What but the black domestic blues is Bessie's lyrical lament that:

> "All my life's been full of hard trouble. If I wasn't hungry, I was sick. And if I wasn't sick, I was in trouble . . . I just worked hard every day as long as I can remember . . . then I had to get drunk to forget it . . . All you ever caused me was trouble, just plain black trouble. All you ever did since we been knowing each other was to get me drunk so's you could have me. That was all! I see it now. I ain't drunk now. I see everything you ever did to me" (pp. 194–195 [215]).

If Bessie had ever been blind, her blues reveal clearly that now she sees all. Wright, who once projected a book on black domestics, was aware of Bessie's blues knowledge. His motion picture version of *Native Son* has a moment in which a blues song that he himself wrote is sung by none other than Bessie Mears.

NOTES

1. Ralph Ellison, *Invisible Man* (New York: Vintage, 1972); Richard Wright, *Native Son* (New York: Harper, 1940). All citations from the novels refer to these editions and are hereafter marked by page numbers in parentheses. For the reader's convenience additional bracketed page references to the Perennial Classic edition of *Native Son* will also be provided.

2. Yi-Fu Tuan, *Space and Place* (Minneapolis: University of Minnesota Press, 1974), p. 6.

3. Michel Fabre and Ellen Wright, eds., *Richard Wright Reader* (New York: Harper and Row, 1978), p. 144. My emphasis.

4. Richard Wright, *12 Million Black Voices: A Folk History of the Negro in the United States* (New York: Viking, 1941; rpt. The New York Times, 1969), p. 11. All citations refer to this edition and are hereafter marked by page numbers in parentheses.

5. In her introduction to *The Body in Pain* (New York: Oxford University Press, 1958), Elaine Scarry says: "Physical pain does not simply resist language but actively destroys it, bringing about an immediate reversion to a state anterior to language, to the sounds and cries a human being makes before language is learned" (p. 4). What is useful about her observation for the present discussion is the implicitly precultural state to which pain reduces its carrier and sufferer. The precultural can be considered, as well, a cultural death. Reduced, stripped of a "language" for a new, agonizing, and horrible pain, the African "gives up" African culture in its pre-pain discursive specificity.

6. In Eric Williams, *Capitalism and Slavery* (New York: Capricorn Books, 1966), p. 35.

7. Ibid., p. 19.

8. Ibid., p. 7.

9. Ibid.

10. Harriet Beecher Stowe, *Uncle Tom's Cabin* (New York: Collier, 1962), p. 74.

11. Pages 68–73 of a 143-page narrative.

12. The observation belongs to Charlotte Pierce-Baker on seeing the huge towers in Chicago that Mayor Jane Byrne moved into for a week in a symbolic show of identification with the inhabitants.

13. "And high above me now the bridge seemed to move off to where I could not see, striding like a robot, an iron man, whose iron legs clanged doomfully as it moved. And then I struggled up, full of sorrow and pain, shouting, 'No, no, we must stop him!'" Ellison, *Invisible Man*, p. 558.

14. Adrienne Rich, *Of Woman Born* (New York: Bantam, 1981), p. 175.

15. Richard Wright, "Blueprint for Negro Writing," in Addison Gayle, Jr., ed., *The Black Aesthetic* (New York: Doubleday, 1971), pp. 333–45. All citations of the essay refer to this version and are hereafter marked by page numbers in parentheses. The essay originally appeared in *New Challenge* in 1937.

16. Bettina Aptheker, *Woman's Legacy: Essays on Race, Sex, and Class in*

American History (Amherst: University of Massachusetts Press, 1982), p. 112. Bare statistics suggest that Wright's perception of an absence of "women in the making" in industry was not exclusively a function of his own imagination. In 1940, only thirteen per cent of black women in the labor force served as either white- or blue-collar workers, while seventy-four per cent of white women served in such capacities. Further, seventy per cent of black women in the labor force served in 1940 as "service workers"; sixty per cent of that number were, in fact, "private household workers."

17. Until 1935 and the Seventh World Congress in Moscow, the Communist Party of the United States endorsed the notion of a black nation within America, calling for "self-determination in the Black Belt" as a goal. The League of Struggle for Negro Rights and the *Negro Liberator* were agencies designed to secure such a nationalist end. With the coming of the Popular Front, however, designed to curb the powers of Nazi Germany and the spread of fascism, the nationalist program for American blacks was abandoned, leading to a sense of betrayal on the part of some black Communist Party supporters. Mark Naison's *Communists in Harlem During the Depression* (New York: Grove, 1983) contains an account of the shifting policies of the CPUSA during the 1930s.

18. Sigmund Freud, *The Interpretation of Dreams* (New York: Avon, 1965), trans. James Strachey, p. 429. All citations from the text refer to this edition and are hereafter marked by page numbers in parentheses.

19. Deborah Gray White, *Ar'n't I A Woman? Female Slaves in the Plantation South* (New York: Norton, 1958), p. 63.

20. Ibid., p. 63.

21. Olaudah Equiano, *The Life of Olaudah Equiano, or Gustavus Vassa, The African Written By Himself,* in Arna Bontemps, ed., *Great Slave Narratives* (Boston: Beacon, 1969), pp. 27, 29.

22. Angela Y. Davis, *Women, Race and Class* (New York: Random House, 1981), pp. 23–24.

23. A paraphrase of Adrienne Rich's *Of Woman Born.*

24. In his still controversial essay in definition of the "protest novel" entitled "Many Thousands Gone," Baldwin writes of a "necessary dimension" that had been excluded from black life by *Native Son* – "this dimension being the relationship that Negroes bear to one another, that depth of involvement and unspoken recognition of shared experience which creates a way of life . . . [with the eradication of this dimension, we are] led . . . to believe that in Negro life there exists no tradition, no field of manners, no possibility of ritual or

intercourse, such as may, for example, sustain the Jew even after he has left his father's house." *Notes of a Native Son* (Boston: Beacon, 1955), pp. 35–36.

25. Karl Marx, *The Eighteenth Brumaire of Louis Bonaparte,* in Lewis S. Feuer, ed., *Writings on Politics and Philosophy* (New York: Anchor, 1959), p. 320.

Bigger's Blues: *Native Son* and the Articulation of Afro-American Modernism

CRAIG WERNER

> There will be time to murder and create
> — "The Love Song of J. Alfred Prufrock"

THE problems are fragmentation, alienation, sense-making: the shoring up of fragments against our ruins; what to make of a diminished thing. Timothy Reiss and Michel Foucault, indispensable genealogists of the "modern," have identified the European origins of these crucial twentieth-century concerns in pre-Enlightenment challenges to the medieval world view. Social, scientific, technological, and theological innovations shape new discourses which in turn generate new insights, in a process Henry Adams labelled the "law of acceleration." One of the earliest Euro-American texts framed in self-consciously modernist terms, *The Education of Henry Adams* was published in 1909, six years after W. E. B. Du Bois's *The Souls of Black Folk*. Du Bois's absence from most discussions of the central aesthetic, intellectual, and cultural issues raised in Euro-American modernism helps explain both the continuing invisibility of Afro-American modernism as a literary movement and the marginalization or simplification of Langston Hughes's "Montage of a Dream Deferred," Zora Neale Hurston's *Moses, Man of the Mountain*, and, crucially, *Native Son*.

Although most of Adams's insights had been anticipated by Melville, Henry and William James, and Emily Dickinson, the publication of *The Education of Henry Adams* serves as a convenient marker for the beginning of modernism as a self-conscious element of literary discourse in the United States. Recognizing the complex continental history behind this relatively late emergence, critics such as Hugh Kenner, Malcolm Bradbury and James

117

McFarlane, and Frederick Karl quite properly have oriented their investigations of Ezra Pound, T. S. Eliot, William Faulkner, and other recognized modernists toward the continental figures and movements which influenced their work. Even the emerging histories of "alternative modernisms" – such as those of Cyrena Pondrum, Sandra Gilbert, Susan Stanford Friedman, Susan Gubar, and Shari Benstock – share this Eurocentric focus. Certainly it would be remiss to discuss Eliot without reference to symbolism, H. D. without reference to Freud, Faulkner without reference to Joyce.

Nonetheless, such approaches create and perpetuate significant lacunae by excluding or marginalizing texts and traditions which cannot adequately be articulated in vocabularies derived from Baudelaire, Freud, Nietzsche, or Joyce. Calling for a historicized view of modernism, Lillian S. Robinson and Lise Vogel's germinal essay "Modernism and History" (1971) addresses the limitations of the traditional New Critical view of modernism as a movement committed to "esthetic inviolability."[1] Robinson and Vogel argue that such an approach both reflects and furthers the politically problematic tendency of modernism "to intensify isolation. It forces the work of art, the artist, the critic, and the audience outside of history. Modernism denies us the possibility of understanding ourselves as *agents* in the material world, for all has been removed to an abstract world of ideas, where interactions can be minimized or emptied of meaning and real consequences."[2] Since the publication of "Modernism and History," the New Critical approach to modernism has been substantially revised in response to a variety of challenges posed by "postmodernists," many of whom adapt the premises of politically aware theorists such as Bertolt Brecht and Michael Bakhtin. Similarly, poststructuralist theory questions the foundations of all oppositional thinking, including the assertion of a division between aesthetics and politics. It seems unlikely that either Robinson or Vogel – who are aware of their scholarship as part of a kinetic process grounded in the particular historical circumstances of the moment of composition – would today be quite so categorical in their political repudiation of modernism.

If much has changed since 1971, much has remained the same. Despite sensitive revisions of "canonical" modernism – particularly Frederick Karl's *Modern and Modernism* – Robinson and Vogel's comment on the Euro- and phallo-centrism of modernism as traditionally defined in academia retains its cogency: "To be conscious of race, class, or sex with respect to high culture is to be conscious, first of all, of exclusion."[3] This remains particularly clear in relation to Afro-American literature. Even as they challenge the hegemony of traditional discourse, many feminist and postmodernist critics – even some who grant attention to individual Afro-American texts or writers – show only a passing acquaintance with the complexity of the cultural traditions informing Afro-American writing.

By considering *Native Son* – usually viewed as a realistic protest (whether ideological or existential) novel – specifically in the matrix of Euro-American modernism, this essay seeks to reclaim access to a modernist tradition compatible with the communal, kinetic, and political (though usually not ideological) imperatives of the Afro-American blues tradition. Several Afro-American critics – most notably Houston Baker, Ralph Ellison, Henry Louis Gates, and Robert Stepto – have identified points of connection between Euro-American theoretical discourse and Afro-American vernacular expression. None is entirely comfortable with Wright's position in that dialogue or, more generally, in the Afro-American literary tradition. Each evinces some discomfort with *Native Son* and prefers to focus on *Black Boy*. In addition to suggesting a revised sense of the modernist movement, approaching *Native Son* as a modernist text helps reassert its position as a central, if problematical, Afro-American text. Standing at the crossroads (to use the term Baker adapts from Robert Johnson, after Johnson had adapted it from the black and unknown bards who preceded him in the New World and the Old) where Afro- and Euro-American traditions intersect, Wright focuses his treatment of fragmentation, alienation, and sense-making on his most powerfully resonant figure of exclusion: Bigger Thomas.

In part because he can articulate his experience fully neither in Afro- nor Euro-American terms – an inability that connects him profoundly with his creator – Bigger has too frequently been undervalued by even Wright's most insightful critics. In the midst of a moving celebration of *Black Boy*, for example, Ellison criticizes Wright for forcing "into Bigger's consciousness concepts and ideas which his intellect could not formulate."[4] Commenting on Bigger's limitations, Ellison wrote: "Wright could imagine Bigger, but Bigger could not possibly imagine Richard Wright. Wright saw to that."[5] Stepto, whose book *From Behind the Veil* follows Ellison in placing *Black Boy* at the center of Wright's canon, pursues the implications of Ellison's critique further, connecting Bigger's limitations with Wright's own. In "I Thought I Knew These People: Richard Wright and the Afro-American Literary Tradition," Stepto observes that "Wright's refusal to partake of the essential intraracial rituals which the situation demanded suggests that he was either unaware of, or simply refused to participate in, those viable modes of speech represented in history by the preacher and orator and in letters by the articulate hero."[6] Stepto is certainly correct in identifying the central issue as "Wright's idea of the hero."[7] Where Stepto accords Bigger a "sub-heroic posture,"[8] however, I would suggest the phrase "pre-heroic posture." Thwarted in his attempts to achieve what Stepto calls ascent – the passage from oppression to a limited freedom based on the attainment of Euro-American literacy – Bigger provides a compelling figure of the internal dynamics of what Stepto calls the "symbolic South."[9] Ironically, it is Bigger's very sense of alienation from the Afro-American community that helps make him such a powerful figure for the part of that community which has not achieved the ascent. While I would agree with Stepto that Wright's sense of alienation places him in "the mainstream of American letters,"[10] a close reading of *Native Son* in relation to the concerns of the modernist current of that mainstream suggests the ways in which his articulation of that alienation places him in the blues-based mainstream of Afro-American letters. Listening carefully to Bigger Thomas's inarticulate blues, we can more easily perceive the modernist blues novel inside the realist protest novel and envision a crossroads meeting of Bigger Thomas with Samuel Beckett, Toni Morrison, or Bertolt Brecht.

Afro-American Culture and the Discourses of Modernism

At least since Du Bois produced *The Souls of Black Folk,* Afro-American culture has explicitly addressed the central concerns of modernism: fragmentation, alienation, sense-making. Du Bois's description of "double consciousness" emphasizes one particular experience of the fragmented world, an experience which alienates the individual from both the disintegrating community and a secure sense of self. According to Du Bois, the Afro-American experiences "a world which yields him no true self-consciousness, but only lets him see himself through the revelation of the other world. It is a peculiar sensation, this double-consciousness, this sense of always looking at one's self through the eyes of others."[11] Contemporary critics such as Stepto and Henry Louis Gates address the ways in which this fragmented world view gives rise to "double" or "multiple" modes of sense-making. Gates's analysis of the Afro-American practice of signifying complements Stepto's sense of distinct types of "literacy" associated with specific situations within American society. Like Charles W. Chesnutt, Zora Neale Hurston, and Ellison, these critics recognize Afro-American expressive practices as intricate adjustments to a world fragmented by the communal experience of slavery and racial oppression. Understood from a Du Boisian perspective, then, the central problem confronted by Afro-American culture closely resembles that confronted by mainstream modernism: the alienated individual experiences a profound sense of psychological and cultural disorientation in a world characterized by an accelerating rate of change; he or she subsequently attempts to regain some sense of coherence by articulating the experience of disorientation. The difference lies in the tendency of many Euro-American modernists to experience their situation as individual and, to some extent, ahistorical, while Afro-American modernists generally perceive a communal dilemma deriving from historical and political forces. It should be noted that this association of racial experience with the modernist sensibility is not limited to Afro-American writers. As Thadious Davis and Eric Sundquist have demonstrated, William Faulkner's use of modernist techniques – in particular, fragmented narrative perspectives – can be traced to his perception of the black–white division of his native Mississippi as well as to his awareness of continental modernist literature.

Despite the general unawareness of Du Boisian double consciousness in discussions of modernism, both traditional and alternative critics have understood modernism as a pervasive cultural dislocation affecting the quality of life not just for artists, but also for those unaware of the historical origins and philosophical implications of their own situations. Paul Fussell's *The Great War and Modern Memory* and Samuel Hynes's *The Auden Generation* identify World War I as the culmination of a long historical process which led to a widespread perception of the world as a moral and psychological "waste land." The postwar malaise seems to have been felt most acutely in urban settings, where the impact of technological advances had been accelerating for nearly a century. The first two major Afro-American literary movements of the century were centered in cities: New York during the Harlem Renaissance of the 1920s and, as Robert Bone has convincingly argued, Chicago during an equally significant but less publicized Chicago Renaissance that included Wright and lasted from the mid 1930s through the early 1950s. It seems particularly noteworthy that one of the major contrasts between the early Harlem Renaissance, particularly as described in Alain Locke's "The New Negro," and the Chicago Renaissance lies in the increasing awareness of the city not as promised land but as an unreal waste land that destroys blacks in particularly vicious ways.

If we align our perspective with that of Bigger Thomas, this urban waste land can be seen as a disorienting texture of competing discourses of equivalent significance. Literary modernism, whatever its particular form, takes its place alongside a number of other discourses, including those of film, advertising, and journalism. Each of these discourses has been viewed as a signal index of the modern world; each excludes Afro-American participation almost entirely. Roland Marchand's brilliant book, *Advertising the American Dream: Making Way For Modernity 1920–1940*, discusses advertising professionals as self-described "apostles of modernity" who saw themselves both responding to and shaping cultural realities as profoundly important as those addressed by Eliot. Competing styles of advertising – as Joyce realized when he placed advertising salesman Leopold Bloom at the center of his epic novel – reflect concerns over the relationship of artist/advertiser to material and audience which parallel those of more traditional artists such as Stephen Dedalus. In *Ulysses* and in Dos Passos's *U.S.A.*, advertising provides a fascinating focal point for examination of the relationship between "high" and "popular" discourses. From Bigger Thomas's viewpoint, however, the claims put forward in the advertising journal *Printers' Ink* are not qualitatively different from those advanced in *Des Imagistes*. The same critique can be applied to Bigger's relationship with practically every other mainstream discourse, whether or not it is immediately available to him in his corner of the waste land.

Wright's presentation of a variety of these discourses – advertising, journalistic, cinematic, legal, aesthetic, Marxist – continually emphasizes Bigger's exclusion. Some of the exclusions are self-evident. The journalistic discourse pictured in *Native Son* contributes directly to Bigger's death. In addition to discovering Mary's body in the furnace, the journalists – and in his presentation Wright was, as Keneth Kinnamon has demonstrated, accurately reporting the actions of the Chicago press during the Nixon case, which provided the background for the novel[12] – convict Bigger of rape in the absence of any evidence and prior to his trial. Although Bigger hopes momentarily that his acts of rebellion will force the newspapers to "carry the story, *his* story,"[13] his continuing exclusion is made clear in the newspaper clipping that tacitly endorses the Jackson, Mississippi, journalist who labels Bigger a "trouble-making nigger" (p. 239 [261]). It hardly seems surprising that a large percentage of references to newspapers in *Native Son* associate journalism with the bloody head of Mary Dalton (pp. 79, 100 [91, 112–113], and many others). Together, Mary's head and the journalistic discourse assure Bigger's death.

Wright presents the movies and advertising in similar terms. Although Bigger looks to the movies for escape from the circumstances of his life (pp. 12, 24 [17, 31]), the movies he sees in *Native Son* simply reiterate his exclusion. *Trader Horn* is a Tarzan-style movie which presents blacks in stereotypical images: "naked . . . whirling in wild dances" (p. 29 [35]); *The Gay Woman* presents equally stereotypical images of upper-class white life. Similarly, the two advertisements Bigger sees early in the "Fear" section combine mockery and direct attack. When he encounters the first – a campaign poster for Buckley, the state's attorney who prosecutes his case – Bigger is aware of a "huge colored poster" showing a "white face" (p. 11 [16]). Despite his limited knowledge of the white world, Bigger clearly recognizes the mockery of the slogan "IF YOU BREAK THE LAW, YOU CAN'T WIN" (p. 11 [16]). Shortly thereafter Bigger and Gus see a skywriting plane "so far away that at times the strong glare of the sun blanked it from sight" (p. 14 [19]). When they are able to decipher the words, the message – "Use Speed Gasoline" (p. 15 [20]) – has little relevance to their lives. In each case, Wright presents a discourse which either mocks or excludes Afro-American experience. When they involve blacks at all – as in the poster advertising *Trader Horn* (p. 25 [32]) or the newspaper photo of Bigger with his "teeth bared in a snarl" (p. 285 [311]) – the discourses perpetuate stereotypical images.

Boris Max comments on the significance of these exclusions when he observes: "How constantly and overwhelmingly the advertisements, radios, newspapers and movies play upon us! But in thinking of them remember that to many they are tokens of mockery. These bright colors may fill our hearts with elation, but to many they are daily taunts. Imagine a man walking amid such a scene, a part of it, and yet knowing that it is *not* for him!" (p. 332 [363]). While Max directs his comments primarily toward popular discourses, his observation is equally applicable to aesthetic and political discourse. When he first enters the Dalton house, Bigger encounters "several paintings whose nature he tried to make out" (p. 39 [47]). Failing to do so, in part because he has been excluded from the cultural heritage of nonrepresentational modernist art, Bigger experiences a rapidly increasing sense of alienation: "strange objects challenged him; and he was feeling angry and uncomfortable" (p. 39 [47]). Wright does not, however, use this scene to endorse the "social realist" aesthetic which had emerged after the suppression of technical experimentation following the Soviet "Silver Age." In *How "Bigger" Was Born*, Wright implies that by the time he began writing *Native Son* the Communist Party leadership had lost all sense of the deconstructive implications of

Marx. As a result, Wright felt a strong pressure to simplify his presentation of Bigger, in effect to exclude aspects of his experience: "How could I create such complex and wide schemes of associational thought and feeling, such filigreed webs of dreams and politics, without being mistaken for a 'smuggler of reaction'?"[14] For the moment, it is sufficient to emphasize that, like the popular discourses, the leading aesthetic discourses of the 1930s exclude important aspects of Bigger's – and Wright's – experience. Nonetheless, the very attempt to include the discourses, or more precisely fragments of these discourses, in the text of *Native Son* highlights Wright's close relationship to a modernism grounded – though Wright would almost certainly not have thought of his work in these terms – in the blues.

The Modernism of *Native Son*

Wright's interest in modernism, well established by the time he wrote *Native Son*, is thoroughly documented. Although his earliest reading focused on American realists and naturalists, he developed a serious interest in the modernist avant-garde soon after he moved to Chicago in the late 1920s. By 1935 he was discussing Eliot, Joyce, and Stein with members of the John Reed and South Side Writers' Clubs. He continued these discussions with Ralph Ellison – later to be recognized as an Afro-American modernist – whom he met after moving to New York in the late 1930s. Writing in the Federal Writers' Project publication *New York Panorama*, Wright observed in obviously self-referential terms that "Joyce's *Ulysses* influenced some of the Negro writers, and even the gospel of Gertrude Stein claimed a number of Negro adherents."[15] More importantly, Wright had experimented extensively with modernist techniques in the fiction and poetry he had written prior to *Native Son*. *Lawd Today*, written during the mid-1930s but published only after Wright's death, is a conscious rewriting of *Ulysses*. Filled with direct allusions to Joyce and Eliot, the novel employs a mythic parallel and multiple styles to catalog one day in the life of a black Chicago postal worker. *Uncle Tom's Children*, Wright's first published book, intentionally recalls *Dubliners*; the final story, "Bright and Morning Star," ends with a direct revoicing of the conclusion

125

of Joyce's "The Dead." In *American Hunger,* Wright describes the aesthetic approach of *Uncle Tom's Children* and his 1930s poetry in terms reminiscent of Eliot's "objective correlative": "My purpose was to capture a physical state or movement that carried a strong subjective impression . . . If I could fasten the mind of the reader upon words so firmly that he would forget words and be conscious only of his response, I felt that I would be in sight of knowing how to write narrative."[16]

Compared to the obvious modernism of Wright's earlier work, *Native Son* appears superficially to be a traditional narrative, especially in formal terms. To dismiss its modernism entirely, however, is to risk repressing a central element of Wright's literary genealogy, and thereby to perpetuate the identification of modernism with a specific set of techniques. Perhaps the clearest mark of *Native Son*'s modernism is Wright's presentation of Chicago as an Afro-American version of Eliot's "unreal city." Echoing Eliot and Carl Sandburg (another Chicago-based writer who saw no necessary contradiction between populist politics and modernist aesthetics), *How "Bigger" Was Born* emphasizes the unresolved tensions of the "fabulous city in which Bigger lived, an indescribable city, huge, roaring, dirty, noisy, raw, stark, brutal; a city of extremes: torrid summers and sub-zero winters, white people and black people, the English language and strange tongues, foreign born and native born, scabby poverty and gaudy luxury, high idealism and hard cynicism!"[17] In his introduction to St. Clair Drake and Horace Cayton's study of Chicago, *Black Metropolis,* Wright elaborates on this "fatal division of being, a war of impulses" he shared with many other black migrants in Chicago: "in that great iron city, that impersonal, mechanical city, amid the steam, the smoke, the snowy winds, the blistering suns; there in that self-conscious city, that city so deadly dramatic and stimulating, we caught whispers of the meanings that life could have, and we were pushed and pounded by facts much too big for us."[18]

While most critics stress the naturalistic quality of the treatment of the city in *Native Son,* Wright tempers his naturalism with a modernist subtext emphasizing the city's psychological impact. Bigger Thomas experiences the city as an entity that is at once living and dead: "There were many empty buildings with black windows, like blind eyes, buildings like skeletons" (p. 147 [163]), and "They stopped in front of a tall, snow-covered building whose many windows gaped blackly, like the eye-sockets of empty skulls" (p. 195 [216]). Recalling the modernist genealogy linking Poe, Baudelaire, and the "Circe" section of *Ulysses*, Wright presents the city as an objective correlative for Bigger's psychological state. The burned-out buildings of the black belt serve as a particularly effective objective correlative for Bigger's situation. Not only do they impose a constant reminder of the waste land, they also recall the racially specific history which excludes Bigger from even the shared experience of fragmentation. Entering one of the collapsing buildings, Bigger sees "walls almost like those of the Dalton home. . . . That was the way most houses on the South Side were, ornate, old, stinking; homes once of rich white people, now inhabited by Negroes or standing dark and empty with yawning black windows" (p. 155 [172]). What from a Euro-American perspective could serve as an emblem of the decay of a once-proud tradition is, from the Afro-American perspective, simply another reminder of the continuity of racial exclusion.

It is hardly surprising that Bigger experiences this waste land in surrealistic terms. Several of Wright's descriptions present the city as a psychic landscape of the type associated with the "metaphysical picaresque," a genre that, as Monique Chefdor has demonstrated, unifies apparently distinct strains of modernism.[19] As Bigger crosses the threshold of the ornate old building with Bessie, the shift in the imagery describing his perception reflects his growing sense of absolute exclusion: "He looked up and down the street, past ghostly lamps that shed a long series of faintly shimmering cones of yellow against the snowy night. He took her to the front entrance which gave into a vast pool of inky silence. He brought out the flashlight and focused the round spot on a rickety stairway leading upward into a still blacker darkness" (p. 155 [171]). The image of the "inky silence" preceding the existential blackness in which he will kill Bessie seems particularly significant given Bigger's exclusion from written discourse. After the murder, Wright emphasizes Bigger's previous experiences of perceptual dislocation, his sense of inhabiting a world where even fundamental laws of physics fail to provide a coherent framework for perception: "never had he felt a sense of wholeness. Sometimes, in his room or on the sidewalk, the world seemed to him a strange labyrinth even when the streets were straight and the walls were square; a chaos which made him feel that something in him should be able to understand it, divide it, focus it" (pp. 203–4 [225]).

The murders of Mary and Bessie bring this long-standing sense of dislocation to a climax. Bigger senses that his violence is inextricably linked to the city in which he lives; each murder is accompanied by a redefinition of Bigger's sense of what the city means. Immediately after realizing that Mary is dead, Bigger experiences the city – imaged as a totally white presence – as an absolute determinant of his actions: "The reality of the room fell from him; the vast city of white people that sprawled outside took its place" (p. 75 [86]). Having crossed the threshold into the metaphysical darkness of the ornate old building, however, his sense of the city undergoes a profound transformation. Immediately before he kills Bessie, he experiences a moment in which "the city did not exist" (p. 199 [221]). Torn between these extremes – experiencing a tension of a sort basic to the modernist sensibility – Bigger gradually realizes that the question is not whether or not the city exists; rather it is what his own consciousness *makes* of the city. Associating the city with the whiteness of the fallen snow, Bigger – like many modernist criminal–artist–metaphysical picaros – begins to explore his own sense-making process: "The snow had stopped falling and the city, white, still, was a vast stretch of roof-tops and sky. He had been thinking about it for hours here in the dark and now there it was, all white, still. But what he had thought about it had made it real with a reality it did not have now in the daylight. When lying in the dark thinking of it, it seemed to have something which left it when it was looked at" (p. 204 [226]).

This ever-changing waste land exerts a profoundly fragmenting impact on Bigger's consciousness. In *How "Bigger" Was Born*, Wright echoes Du Bois's analysis of double consciousness when he traces the Afro-American sense of fragmentation to the existence of "two worlds, the white world and the black world." The split is as much psychological as political, because "the very tissue of [Afro-Americans'] consciousness received its tone and timbre from the strivings of that dominant civilization." Aggravating the racially specific problem for Bigger is the fact that even the dominant civilization had come to perceive itself as a waste land. Wright observes that Bigger is a "product of a dislocated society; he is a dispossessed and disinherited man; he is all of this, and he lives amid the greatest possible plenty on earth and he is looking and feeling for a way out."[20] Although Wright pursues the implications of this observation in specifically political terms, the description would serve as well for Eliot's J. Alfred Prufrock. Like his modernist contemporaries, Bigger experiences a profound sense of entrapment emanating from a confusion of subjective and objective that subverts his sense of self. Just as the city assumes an organic quality, other people repeatedly lose their human solidity, casting Bigger adrift in a world of semianimate barriers. Mary and Jan seem "two vast white looming walls" (p. 59 [68]). When he is captured, Bigger looks out at "a circle of white faces; but he was outside of them, behind his curtain, his wall" (p. 228 [252]). In this context, the similarity between the modernist malaise and Du Boisian double consciousness seems clear. Both alienate the individual from any unified sensibility. Throughout *Native Son*, Bigger feels his own fragmentation: "He was divided and pulled against himself" (p. 21 [27]); "There were two Biggers" (p. 214 [236–7]). Such division seems the inevitable response to a context in which every word, every symbol possesses at least two – and frequently many more – possible meanings. The cross of the preachers and the cross of the Ku Klux Klan dissolve into one another in Bigger's fragmented consciousness (p. 287 [313]). Although he lacks words to express his sense of this fragmentation – and in this he is as much modernist artist/hero as the inarticulate victim described by Ellison – Bigger is acutely aware of his own lack of wholeness: "never in all his life, with this black skin of his, had the two worlds, thought and feeling, will and mind, aspiration and satisfaction, been together; never had he felt a sense of wholeness" (pp. 203–4 [225]). As he prepares for death, Bigger's apprehension of his fragmentation takes the form of an intensely solipsistic speculation which would not be out of place in a Beckett mindscape: "If he were nothing, if this were all, then why could not he die without hesitancy? Who and what was he to feel the agony of a won-

129

der so intensely that it amounted to fear? Why was this strange impulse always throbbing in him when there was nothing outside of him to meet it and explain it? Who or what had traced this restless design in him? Why was this eternal reaching for something that was not there? Why this black gulf between him and the world: warm red blood here and cold blue sky there, and never a wholeness, a oneness, a meeting of the two?" (p. 350–1 [383]).

Bigger's internal response to his fragmentation, like those of "metaphysical picaros" from Leopold Bloom to Tyrone Slothrop of *Gravity's Rainbow*, passes through several distinct phases. Gradually, Bigger's initial disorientation gives way to an exhilarating sense of himself as questing hero, which in turn disintegrates into a solipsistic sense of total meaninglessness, differing from the original situation because previously Bigger had been unaware of even the possibility of meaning. The final stage of Bigger's metaphysical wandering, explicitly recalling Eliot's "The Love Song of J. Alfred Prufrock," involves a direct confrontation with the association of criminal and artist in the modernist sensibility, an extended meditation on what it means "to murder and create."

At the outset of *Native Son*, Bigger embodies, to use Wright's phrase from *How "Bigger" Was Born*, "a hot and whirling vortex of undisciplined and unchannelized impulses."[21] His perception oscillates wildly between extreme subjectivity and extreme objectivity: "The sharp precision of the world of steel and stone dissolved into blurred waves. He blinked and the world grew hard again, mechanical, distinct" (p. 14 [19]). Similar feelings of being cast adrift in a discontinuous world recur throughout the novel. Confronting the journalists in the Dalton basement, Bigger feels that "Events were like the details of a tortured dream, happening without cause. At times it seemed that he could not quite remember what had gone before and what it was he was expecting to come" (p. 169 [187]). Paralyzed by this Dostoevskian "deadlock of impulses" which renders him "unable to rise to the land of the living" (p. 83 [93]), Bigger experiences himself as a cipher, surrendering all sense of control to the mechanical world around him: "He was not driving; he was simply sitting and floating along smoothly through darkness" (p. 67 [77–8]).

This feeling of ease, of course, collapses almost immediately, leaving Bigger with only the darkness. His growing awareness of alienation, however, marks the beginning of a significant new stage of Bigger's metaphysical journey. Whereas in the "Fear" section Bigger seems unaware of the relationship between external and internal experience, in "Flight" he senses the importance of sense-making processes to the construction of reality. This recognition begins as a vague desire to resist being defined by the discourses which surround him. In a sequence of passages recalling Pound's imagist principle of "Direct presentation of the 'thing,' whether subjective or objective," Bigger "wished that he could be an idea in their minds" (p. 110 [123]). At several points, he immerses himself directly in a level of experience which strips away the verbal discourse – the Eliotic "babble of voices" (p. 184 [204]) – that surrounds him: "The world of sound fell abruptly away from him and a vast picture appeared before his eyes, a picture teeming with so much meaning that he could not react to it all at once" (p. 116 [129–30]). Bigger enters this new realm of experience with a feeling of exhilaration grounded on an unfamiliar sense of his own significance: "he held within the embrace of his bowels the swing of planets through space" (p. 151 [167]).

This sense of liberation from external discourses, however, generates its own countermovement, plunging Bigger into solipsistic isolation. An extreme, and dangerous, separation from the external social realities that condition his consciousness accompanies Bigger's growing awareness of the world of images: "He had been so deeply taken up with his own thoughts that he did not know if he had actually heard anything or had imagined it" (p. 162 [179]). As the external forces reassert their power, Bigger struggles to maintain a grasp on his internal reality, which Wright images increasingly in terms of total isolation. Staring into the airshaft of the old ornate building, Bigger projects his sense of desolation: "He looked downward and saw nothing but black darkness into which now and then a few flakes of white floated from the sky" (p. 196 [217]). Again, the description suggests Beckett. Echoing the Faulkner of *The Sound and the Fury,* Wright associates this landscape with Bigger's experience of a meaninglessness which he feels all the more intensely for his dawning sense of his own significance: "Outside in the cold night the wind moaned and died down, like an idiot in an icy black pit" (p. 200 [221]).

As his treatment of Bigger's subsequent metaphysical wandering demonstrates, however, Wright does not simply abandon his metaphysical picaro to a waste land "signifying nothing." Rather, Wright emphasizes Bigger's attempt to wrest meaning from his isolation. The final section of *Native Son* can be seen as a gloss on the line from "The Love Song of J. Alfred Prufrock" that provides the epigraph for this essay: "There will be time to murder and create." Wright alludes directly to Eliot's line several times, first near the start of the "Flight" section – "He had murdered and had created a new life for himself" (p. 90 [101]) – and again near its end – "He had committed murder twice and had created a new world for himself" (pp. 204–5 [226]). Both claims, however, are premature, based on the momentary exhilaration associated with Bigger's discovery of his own significance. When the power of the external world is reasserted in the capture scene, Bigger's sense of creative power vanishes almost entirely. At the beginning of the "Fate" section, Bigger is back in a waste land where even the murders lack meaning. Recalling Eliot's ironic treatment of rebirth imagery in *The Waste Land*, Wright underlines Bigger's despair: "He had reached out and killed and had not solved anything, so why not reach inward and kill that which had duped him? This feeling sprang up of itself, organically, automatically; like the rotted hull of a seed forming the soil in which it should grow again" (p. 234 [255]).

Faced with this dead end, Bigger gradually recaptures the perception which had first emerged during the early stages of his metaphysical quest. Confronted by the babble of voices in his jail cell, he focuses on the relatively unmediated images which resist or redefine the excluding discourses: "there appeared before him a vast black silent void and the images of the preacher swam in that void, grew large and powerful; familiar images which his mother had given him when he was a child at her knee; images which in turn aroused impulses long dormant, impulses that he had suppressed and sought to shunt from his life. They were images which had once given him a reason for living, had explained the world.

132

Now they sprawled before his eyes and seized his emotions in a spell of awe and wonder" (p. 241 [263]). Anticipating the blues emphasis which emerges in the final section of the novel, this reimmersion in images inspires Bigger to recapitulate the earlier stages of his picaresque journey. Recalling the "sense of exclusion that was as cold as a block of ice," Bigger reiterates his awareness of the insufficiency of external discourse: "To those who wanted to kill him he was not human, not included in that picture of Creation." This in turn allows him to recapture his sense of potential creativity, now phrased with an increased awareness of the power of the external world: "that was why he had killed it. To live, he had created a new world for himself, and for that he was to die" (p. 242 [264]). This more complex apprehension of the connection between murder and creation drives Bigger back into himself: "He lived in a thin, hard core of consciousness" (p. 305 [333]). At this stage, he is aware of his solipsism as a conscious choice, a final stage of the Beckettesque metaphysical journey toward confrontation with his own death: "To accustom his mind to death as much as possible, he made all the world beyond his cell a vast grey land where neither night nor day was, peopled by strange men and women whom he could not understand" (p. 349 [381–2]). Nor – and this is very much to the point in regard to the alienation of both Wright and Bigger – could they understand him.

Sense-making and the Form of *Native Son*

In part because of the influence of Ellison's description of Bigger as "a near sub-human indictment of white oppression,"[22] Bigger's sense-making process – the crucial element which connects him with the modernist artist–outsiders – has attracted little attention. Wright contributed substantially to this oversight by constantly reiterating Bigger's inarticulateness. The following passage typifies Wright's comments on Bigger: "Though he could not have put it into words, he felt that . . ." (p. 235 [257]). Similarly, in *How "Bigger" Was Born*, Wright explicitly denies that Bigger possesses any capacity which might be construed as artistic: "Bigger did not offer in his life any articulate verbal explanations."[23] Wright offers this comment in part as justification of his decision to "fall back upon my own feelings as a guide" in the presentation of Bigger, implicitly seconding Ellison's emphasis on the distance between creator and character. Nonetheless, a deep connection exists between Bigger's struggles to articulate, and perhaps communicate, his experience and Wright's analogous struggles, which are reflected in the formal irresolution of *Native Son*. Both Wright and Bigger inhabit a world which offers no vocabulary capable of expressing the particular Afro-American experience of the modernist situation. Nonetheless, both struggle to articulate their experience despite profound problems regarding their relationship to their audiences, both real and potential. Although Bigger and Wright share strong doubts concerning the validity and utility of Afro-American vernacular traditions, both emerge from *Native Son* as blues artists of profound, if ironically tinged, power.

Wright identifies several environmental and psychological causes for Bigger's inarticulateness, reinforcing the view of Bigger as lacking in essential human resources. Wright traces Bigger's alienation to an environmentally determined repression of thought and feeling. Bigger's refusal to acknowledge the emotional reality of his family's suffering is presented as a self-protective strategy grounded in his feeling "that they were suffering and that he was powerless to help them. He knew that the moment he allowed himself to feel to its fulness how they lived, the shame and misery of their lives, he would be swept out of himself with fear and despair" (p. 9 [13]). Similarly, his feeling of impotence in the face of vast environmental pressures stunts his intellectual perception: "But what could he do? Each time he asked himself that question his mind hit a blank wall and he stopped thinking" (p. 11 [16]). Bigger's repression of the reality of his own experience, which would in any case preclude a comprehensive articulation, is reinforced by external factors throughout *Native Son*. Both whites and blacks encourage, and enforce, Bigger's repressed silence. The Mississippi newspaper editor exemplifies white attitudes when he observes that the effectiveness of the southern system rests on "regulating [blacks'] speech and actions" (p. 240 [261]). Even the relatively sympathetic Boris Max contributes to the problem when he tells Bigger, "You won't have to say anything here" (p. 265 [290]) and later informs the court that "he does not wish to testify here" (p. 279 [304]). Similarly, Bigger's family — whom he images as "inarticulate and unconscious" (p. 91 [102]) — and friends discourage his attempts at articulation. When Bigger begins to question the social structure of Chicago, Gus dismisses his words: "Aw, nigger, quit thinking about it. You'll go nuts" (p. 17 [23]). As both politically and psychologically oriented critics have emphasized, Bigger's environment places crushing pressure on the development of his perceptions.

In addition to the environmental factors, *Native Son* suggests a more elusive aspect of the problem of articulation. Beginning with the opening pages of *How "Bigger" Was Born*, Wright intimates a basic inability of language to communicate experience. Focusing on his *own* problems as a writer trying to articulate Bigger's experience, Wright reveals a profound connection with the character incapable of offering "articulate verbal expressions." Three times within the first two pages, Wright describes his frustration over an inability to articulate his own process: "Always there is something that is just beyond the tip of the tongue that could explain it all"; "the author is eager to explain. But the moment he makes the attempt his words falter"; "he is left peering with eager dismay back into the dim reaches of his own incommunicable life."[24] That almost all modernist writers experience a similar frustration is precisely the point: Bigger Thomas's struggle to render his experience in words is only more extreme than — not qualitatively different from — that which led Yeats to create the private language of *Mythologies* or Joyce to write *Finnegans Wake*.

The problem lies not only with the environment but with the difficulty of articulation per se, a difficulty that lies near the foundation of postmodernist literature and poststructuralist theory. The situation for Wright was particularly problematic given the obvious inadequacy of Euro-American discourses for the expression of Afro-American experience. That Bigger Thomas senses this makes his struggle for articulation all the more significant. At the start of the novel, Bigger shapes his expression in such a way as to repress feeling. When Mary questions him at the Kitchen Shack, Bigger "groped for neutral words, words that would convey information but not indicate any shade of his own feelings" (p. 63 [73]). In part because his attempts to exert even such limited control over his expression fail, Bigger occasionally arrives at startlingly clear insights into the nature of discourse. Contemplating the social segregation which breeds double consciousness, Bigger realizes that the white power structure conditions all discourse: "As long as he and his black folks did not go beyond certain limits, there was no need to fear that white force. But whether they feared it or not, each and every day of their lives they lived with it; even when words did not sound its name, they acknowledged its reality" (p. 97 [109]). After the murders, Bigger's sense of the "white force" which frustrates his attempts at articulation focuses as much on the inadequacy of the forms of discourse as on external oppressive forces. This sense intervenes when he is confronted by Buckley: "he could never tell why he had killed. It was not that he did not really want to tell, but the telling of it would have involved an explanation of his entire life" (pp. 261–2 [286]). A similar despair over the inadequacy of language, coupled with a haunting intimation of an alternative discourse, recurs when Bigger speaks with Max: "he knew that the moment he tried to put his feelings into words, his tongue would not move . . . . he wondered wistfully if there was not a set of words which he had in common with others, words which would evoke in others a sense of the same fire that smoldered in him" (pp. 308–309 [337]).

The search for such words – Bigger's desire "to say something to ease the swelling in his chest" (p. 31 [38]) – exerts a profound influence on both the thematic content and the formal structure of *Native Son*. Bigger tells his story, or attempts to tell his story, repeatedly, at first for reasons of self-defense but increasingly in order to address his sense of fragmentation. His first response upon realizing that Mary is dead focuses on the necessity of articulation: "He had to construct a case for 'them' " (p. 75 [86–7]). While self-defense remains an important element of Bigger's later attempts to shape his story, he soon recognizes articulation as a potentially more active form of resistance designed to subvert dominant discourses: "They wanted him to draw the picture and he would draw it like he wanted it. He was trembling with excitement. In the past had they not always drawn the picture for him? He could tell them anything he wanted and what could they do about it?" (p. 135 [149]). After his imprisonment, Bigger moves even farther toward the modernist concept of art as salvation. Struggling for a mode of articulation entirely free of the dominant discourses, he envisions "a vast configuration of images and symbols whose magic and power could lift him up and make him live so intensely that the dread of being black and unequal would be forgotten" (p. 234 [256]).

Alongside this developing sense of the significance of articulation, Wright portrays what amounts to an aesthetic evolution in Bigger's craft. When he first attempts to tell his story, Bigger's approach is almost entirely realistic: "He went over the story again, fastening every detail firmly in his mind" (p. 108 [120]). This emphasis on the concrete entails a belief in the story as fixed form: "he would have to go into details and he would try to fasten hard in his mind the words he spoke so that he could repeat them a thousand times, if necessary" (p. 131 [145]). Such an emphasis on precise rendition of external facts, however, fails to address the actual complexity of Bigger's situation. On the one hand, he comes to realize that any adequate articulation must take into account the subjective as well as the objective. Questioned by Buckley, he "wondered how he could link up his bare actions with what he had felt; but his words came out flat and dull. White men were looking at him, waiting for his words, and all the feelings of his body vanished, just as they had when he was in the car between Jan and Mary" (p. 263 [287]). During the final stage of Bigger's metaphysical journey, after his conviction renders the utilitarian purposes of articulation nearly irrelevant, Wright highlights the increasing subjectivity of Bigger's approach to articulation: "In him again, imperiously, was the desire to talk, to tell; his hands were lifted in mid-air and when he spoke he tried to charge into the tone of his words what he *himself* wanted to hear, what *he* needed" (pp. 354–5 [388]).

Although his awareness of the subjective element of sense-making increases greatly, Bigger never values articulation simply as solipsistic monolog. In large part because his story-telling process originates in the need for self-defense, Bigger is acutely aware of his audiences, shaping distinct versions of his story for Peggy (p. 109 [122]), Bessie (pp. 120 [133], 192 [213]), Britten and Mr. Dalton (p. 143 [158]), Buckley (p. 260 [284]), and Max (p. 296

[323]). Even during his trial, when it becomes apparent that his story will not save his life, Bigger continues to perceive audience as a vital element of articulation. Examining the connection between subjective and external realities — "How could he find out if this feeling of his was true, if others had it?" — Bigger defines his sense of wholeness, of adequate articulation, in terms of contact: "in that touch, response of recognition, there would be union, identity; there would be a supporting oneness, a wholeness which had been denied him all his life" (p. 307 [335]). As his execution nears, Bigger finds it difficult to maintain any belief in the possibility of such contact: "Why this black gulf between him and the world: warm red blood here and cold blue sky there, and never a wholeness, a oneness, a meeting of the two?" (p. 351 [383]). Despite his alienation from Max and his feeling that "What he wanted to say was stronger in him when he was alone" (p. 352 [385]), Bigger attempts to combine subjective intensity and external contact in his final conversation with Max.

The failure of Bigger's attempt to communicate with Max — "He could not talk" (p. 353 [386]) — underscores the insufficiency of modernist discourses for the articulation of Afro-American experience. The failure results most immediately from Max's inability to recognize the seriousness of Bigger's gesture: "Max did not know, had no suspicion of what he wanted, of what he was trying to say" (p. 353 [386]). Reflecting the limitations of the Marxist analysis presented in the "Guilt of the Nation" speech, which reduces Bigger to a victimized "symbol, a test symbol" (p. 324 [354]), Max shows little sense of the complexity of Bigger's consciousness, responding only with "a casual look, devoid of the deeper awareness that Bigger sought" (p. 353 [386]). More importantly, Max's failure to respond increases Bigger's sense of exclusion from the entire world of Euro-American discourse: "Was there any way to break down this wall of isolation? Distractedly, he gazed about the cell, trying to remember where he had heard words that would help him. He could recall none. He had lived outside of the lives of men. Their modes of communication, their symbols and images, had been denied him" (p. 353 [386]).

This sense of exclusion points to a profoundly significant connection between the "inarticulate" Bigger Thomas and the eloquent Richard Wright, a connection readily discernible in the formal characteristics of *Native Son*. Both character and author engage in serious attempts to articulate to the multiple, and frequently threatening, audiences of the fragmented modernist world the connection between subjective and objective experience. Wright's description of Bigger's momentary insight serves as an emblem of his own attempts to communicate: "What was the use of running away? He ought to stop right here in the middle of the sidewalk and shout out what this was. It was so wrong that surely all the black people round him would do something about it; so wrong that all the white people would stop and listen" (p. 211 [233]). Thematically, Wright emphasizes that the difficulty of realizing this vision drives Bigger Thomas towards an anguished solipsism (although, as I shall demonstrate, this is not Bigger's final position). In its superficially traditional narrative voice which conceals a multitude of unresolved modernist tensions – most notably that between Bigger as character/subject and Wright as objective narrator – *Native Son* suggests that, even as he attempted to shout out the truth, Wright sensed the inevitable frustration of his own attempts.

Like Bigger's, Wright's attempts at articulation took place in the context of the historical exclusion of Afro-Americans from the Euro-American "modes of communication," the "symbols and images" of the dominant discourses. Like the Joyce who employed a different style for each chapter of *Ulysses*, or the Pound who assumed innumerable voices in the *Cantos*, Wright responded to the problem in a distinctly modernist way. Summarizing the critical consensus concerning the defining characteristics of modernist form, Ricardo Quinones lists "a determination to look at events from radically shifting points of view, the close juxtaposition of references from different areas of experience (the lofty as well as the banal, the Dionysian as well as the Apollonian), the evolution of character types whose register is complex enough to contain these rapidly shifting emotional, imagistic and lexical changes, and finally the location of this complex of emotional interrelations in a setting that is decidedly cosmopolitan (and polyglot), urban, industrial, and even technological."[25] Some of these elements are immediately obvious in *Native Son*. However, the critical failure to recognize Bigger as a character type of sufficient complexity has combined with Wright's use of realistic techniques – a superficially consistent third-person limited point of view and an emphasis on concrete external details – to obscure the fact that *Native Son* incorporates a modernist form reflecting Wright's "determination to look at events from radically shifting points of view." Nonetheless, the text is filled with competing – and essentially unresolved – perspectives. The fact that many of these violate the realistic surface of the novel – the simultaneous presence of family, friends, lawyer, prosecutor, friends of the victim in Bigger's prison cell is the clearest example – can be traced to the modernist impulses at work in Wright's sensibility. The same principle holds in relation to the lengthy speeches which dominate the "Fate" section. Rather than simple failures of judgment, these speeches represent Wright's attempt to incorporate the range of discourses conditioning Bigger's experience. Max's voice competes with Buckley's; the newspapers propagate the voice of the Ku Klux Klan; a multitude of voices echoes in Bigger's head. Wright offers no more trustworthy center for interpretation than his Euro-American modernist contemporaries.

Bigger's Blues

Recognizing the modernist dimension of *Native Son* leads to the question of why Wright chose not to employ an obviously modernist form such as that of *Lawd Today*. One of the least discussed scenes in *Native Son* – that centering on the figure of the screaming prisoner who commands Bigger's attention before he is strait-jacketed and removed from the cell block – suggests an interesting approach to this issue. Adding to the montage of voices in "Fear," the prisoner – clearly a voice from the margins of American society – introduces the type of articulate black perspective absent from the rest of the text. His summary of conditions on the South Side, cataloging crowded living conditions, poor quality food, exploitative prices, poor schooling and medical care, parallels that offered by Max in his defense of Bigger. Yet when the man screams obsessively about the loss of papers concerning these white crimes which he threatens to "publish . . . to the whole world" (p. 291 [317]), he is rejected as "balmy" by both white captors and black prisoners. "Turning and twisting in the white men's hands," he is "trying desperately to free himself" (p. 290 [317]).

In many ways, the crazy prisoner can be seen as Wright's representation of himself in *Native Son*. Despite his essentially accurate insights into the nature of Afro-American experience, his listeners misapprehend or simply dismiss his words. His failure results both from his blackness and from his refusal to separate intellectual insight and emotional intensity. Conditioned by the inadequacy of existing discourses — an inadequacy against which both Euro- and Afro-American modernists rebelled — his audience is unable to respond to the underlying power of his insights: "Bigger watched, fascinated, fearful. He had the sensation that the man was too emotionally wrought up over whatever it was that he had lost. Yet the man's emotions seemed real; they affected him, compelling sympathy" (p. 291 [318]). The form, rather than the content, of the prisoner's words subverts the communication he desires. If my suggestion that the prisoner provides an image of Wright's aesthetic situation — screaming out to an uncomprehending audience in a multilevelled prison — is accurate, then it seems particularly significant that he is imaged as Bigger's double: "He was about Bigger's size. Bigger had the queer feeling that his own exhaustion formed a hair-line upon which his feelings were poised" (p. 291 [318]). Clearly, this suggests a potential connection between Bigger and his more articulate counterpart. But so long as the prisoner articulates his emotional and intellectual insights in a disjunctive manner, there seems little possibility of real contact between the two.

The relevance of this passage to Wright's rejection of modernist form in *Native Son* seems clear. To employ a modernist form would have been to relinquish the possibility of an audience, of the contact which Wright consistently images as crucial to full articulation. Speaking from the margins of Euro-American discourse, Wright could not risk further marginalization. Like Bigger Thomas, who begins to articulate his experience as a matter of self-defense, Wright could not afford — as a matter of practical survival in an intensely racist culture — to assume a solipsistic stance and declare the audience unreal, irrelevant.

As a result, he was forced to confront a recurring — and still

141

unresolved – problem concerning the relationship between the modernist artist and his or her audience. The most common Euro-American response to the problem has been incisively presented in Charles Baxter's essay "Assaulting the Audience in Modernism," which argues that for the modernist artist "the consumer of art becomes the adversary, no matter what his or her class may be." Baxter traces this adversarial attitude to an attempt "to restore the artist's authority."[26] In its typical modernist forms, this elevation of artistic sovereignty encourages the solipsistic stance which Wright, in large part because of his racial experience, found untenable. Unwilling to surrender either his modernist sensibility or his determination to reach a real audience, Wright found himself marginalized.

Wright was not entirely devoid of modernist allies. During the early 1930s many of the young English writers discussed in Hynes's *The Auden Generation* envisioned a leftist modernism. Elsewhere, John Dos Passos, William Carlos Williams, and Bertolt Brecht shared Wright's desire to create a voice capable of integrating modernist technique and social commitment. Responding to the influential, if formally conservative, leftist critic Georg Lukács, Brecht asserted that realism had developed as an expression of bourgeois society and that a modernism grounded in vernacular forms was the inevitable, if not yet fully developed, voice of the forces which would ultimately lead to the emergence of a dominant proletariat: "Reality changes; in order to represent it, modes of representation must change."[27] For Brecht, this dictated the development of a leftist modernism which would be popular in the sense that it would be "intelligible to the broad masses, adopting and enriching their forms of expression, assuming their standpoint, confirming and correcting it."[28] There is no evidence, however, that Wright was familiar with Brecht's theoretical writing, which attained widespread circulation in English only after World War II. Even if he had known it, it is likely that Wright would have experienced it as yet another form of European discourse which took Afro-American experience insufficiently into account. Still, the general parallel between Wright and Brecht is instructive. Both writers take the audience much more seriously than the majority of their Anglo-American modernist contemporaries; both resist the leftist repudiation of modernist techniques; both turn to vernacular expression – popular or folk culture – as a means of resolving their aesthetic dilemmas.

Where Brecht openly embraced popular forms, however, Wright felt a deep sense of ambivalence. Although he occasionally wrote blues poetry ("Red Clay Blues," "The FB Eye Blues"), Wright never settled on a clear attitude toward Afro-American vernacular music. Perhaps his most famous rejection of the tradition occurs in *Black Boy:* "after the habit of reflection had been born in me, I used to mull over the strange absence of real kindness in Negroes, how unstable was our tenderness, how lacking in genuine passion we were, how void of great hope, how timid our joy, how bare our traditions. . . . I brooded upon the cultural barrenness of black life."[29] Ellison and Stepto have discussed at length the paradoxical irrelevance of the passage to the "blues life" presented in the text. The importance of the passage lies not in what it says about Afro-American culture, but in what it says about the depth of Wright's feeling of exclusion. Although Wright demonstrates a greater appreciation of vernacular expression elsewhere, the underlying ambivalence articulated in *Black Boy* remains a consistent thread in his thought. His essay "Blueprint for Negro Writing" presents folk expression as the strongest existing expression of "the collective sense of Negro life in America,"[30] even as Wright emphasizes the limitations of its implicitly nationalistic political stance. Similarly, Wright's ambivalence toward vernacular forms can be seen in his description of Bigger Thomas, who is described in *How "Bigger" Was Born* as "a Negro nationalist in a vague sense" but "not nationalist enough to feel the need of religion or the folk culture of his own people."[31]

Even Wright's appreciations of folk culture reflect a somewhat simplified sense of Afro-American vernacular aesthetics, particularly in regard to music. Wright's introduction to Paul Oliver's *Blues Fell This Morning,* for example, presents the blues as a form of cultural compensation that excludes major areas of experience. Interpreting the blues as a response to an oppressive racist system which had systematically "nullified" African forms of expression, Wright describes its limitations: "a vocabulary terser than Basic English, shorn of all hyperbole, purged of metaphysical implications, wedded to a frankly atheistic vision of life, and excluding almost all references to nature and her various moods."[32] Even Wright's most moving description of the blues, included in *12 Million Black Voices*, images it in terms of stasis rather than kinetic process: "The ridiculousness and sublimity of love are captured in our blues, those sad-happy songs that laugh and weep all in one breath, those mockingly tender utterances of a folk imprisoned in steel and stone."[33] Comparing these descriptions with the richly metaphysical and distinctly hyperbolic lyrics of Robert Johnson's "Stones in My Passway," "Hellhound on My Trail," and "Me and the Devil Blues" or the natural meditation of Bessie Smith's "Backwater Blues" reveals the limitations of Wright's perspective. Deeply grounded in an essentially religious sensibility – Johnson speaks of damnation, *not* atheism – the blues (as Ellison, Greil Marcus in *Mystery Train*, and Lawrence Levine in *Black Culture and Black Consciousness* have demonstrated) directly addresses a wide range of metaphysical concerns, though certainly not in the vocabulary of Euro-American theological discourse.

Wright's misapprehension of the connection between the blues and gospel, which complement one another to form the kind of comprehensive world view he finds absent, in turn generates the second major limitation in his view of vernacular aesthetics. Both in the foreword to Oliver's book and in the text of *Native Son*, Wright presents black music as essentially passive. Anticipating Ron Karenga's 1960s repudiation of the blues as an "invalid" form expressing "resignation,"[34] Wright associates the blues with "renounced rebellious impulses," emphasizing the form's "passivity, almost masochistic in quality."[35] This description sounds the keynote of the treatment of Afro-American vernacular culture in *Native Son*. For Bigger, folk music does not even offer momentary compensation for or escape from oppression. When his mother sings, "the song irked him" (p. 9 [14]); when Mary Dalton sings "Swing Low, Sweet Chariot" (p. 66 [77]), he feels the song as a direct mockery. Bigger's alienation reflects Wright's view of folk expression as politically passive. Listening to a church congregation singing "Steal Away," Bigger thinks that "the music sang of surrender, resignation" (p. 215 [237]). The self-demeaning interaction of Reverend Hammond and his mother with the whites in Bigger's jail cell reinforces such attitudes.

There are several problems with Wright's presentation of folk aesthetics. Despite his sensitivity to the ironies and ambiguities of modernist writing, Wright seems almost entirely deaf to the double meanings of Afro-American song. From Du Bois and Zora Neale Hurston to the present, Afro-American critics have been acutely aware that the experience of double consciousness had shaped an expressive tradition in which a self-protective surface acceptable to white listeners masked subversive, frequently political, meanings discernible primarily to black listeners. Thus "Steal Away" and "Swing Low" can be heard either as purely religious songs expressing a passive yearning for eternal salvation or as implicitly political messages calling on slaves to escape from their bondage. Such double messages – exploited by Paul Laurence Dunbar in his "Ante-Bellum Sermon" and James Weldon Johnson in "Let My People Go" – highlight the potential for resistance of the Afro-American church, a potential which has been tapped very effectively by Martin Luther King and the Southern Christian Leadership Conference. Grounded in the intense sense of community created in the Afro-American church, this political potential makes the exclusion of the "damned" blues singer even more significant. Not only is he excluded from the dominant white world, he also feels excluded from the vital core of the Afro-American community.

Yet – and this touches on the underlying source of the blues power in *Native Son* – this exclusion is more apparent than real. On the one hand, the blues, like all forms of Afro-American secular music, derives its aesthetic and formal characteristics directly from sacred forms such as the spirituals and gospel. As Amiri Baraka observes in *Blues People*, the AAB form of the classic blues stanza encodes the call and response forms common to slave spirituals, modern gospel music, and work songs. The significance of this form lies in its ability to connect individual and communal experience. In the original forms, the leader of the congregation or work group would sing a line, which would be repeated by the members of the group, who should be understood as collaborators rather than an "audience" in the Euro-American sense. Given the validation of the response, the leader then comments on the issue or experience raised in the initial call. Since many of the "call" lines are grounded in the communal experiences expressed in earlier songs, the call and response dynamic validates the individual, who is able to articulate his or her experience in communally valid forms even in a world at best indifferent and at worst openly hostile to such efforts. Transformed into the individual AAB form of the blues, the call and response dynamic both encodes the possibility of communal–individual contact – precisely the aspect of articulation Wright found modernist discourse unable to accommodate – and emphasizes a reality. This profound feeling of exclusion, juxtaposed with the sense of a lost former world where things had not yet fallen apart, marks the crossroads where the blues and modernism meet in the Afro-American tradition.

This suggests why, despite Wright's personal ambivalence, his work has consistently inspired some of the deepest insights into the literary use of the blues. Wright does not speak *about* the blues; he speaks the blues. Both the definition of the blues advanced in the introduction to *Blues Fell This Morning* – "All blues are a lusty, lyrical realism charged with taut sensibility"[36] – and the previously quoted passage from *12 Million Black Voices* pale beside Ellison's classic description of the blues as "an impulse to keep the painful details and episodes of a brutal experience alive in one's aching consciousness, to finger its jagged grain, and to transcend it, not by the consolation of philosophy but by squeezing from it a near-tragic, near-comic lyricism. As a form, the blues is an autobiographical chronicle of personal catastrophe expressed lyrically."[37] Combined with Ellison's often-reiterated awareness of the metaphysical density and paradoxical imagery of blues performance, this description of Wright's *Black Boy* provides a much more satisfactory approach to Afro-American vernacular aesthetics than anything Wright ever *consciously* articulated. Nor is it surprising to find that the most significant extension of Ellison's definition – that included in Houston Baker's *Blues, Ideology, and Afro-American Literature: A Vernacular Theory* – relies heavily on Wright (as well as on Ellison). Articulating the impact of economic forces on Afro-American aesthetics in the vocabulary of poststructuralist literary theory,

Baker uses "The Man Who Lived Underground" to discuss the way in which Wright employs the *difference* between Euro- and Afro-American discourse to generate a powerful sense of "the vision and feeling of a *black blues life*."[38]

While Ellison, Baker, and Stepto (who presents *Black Boy* as both a response to previous Afro-American expression and a call for subsequent writers) all recognize Wright's importance to the tradition of blues literature, it seems curious that none focus their discussions on *Native Son*. Nonetheless, *Native Son* remains for many readers, including myself, Wright's most deeply felt vision of the black blues life, combining Ellison's sense of vernacular aesthetics with Baker's awareness of the ideology of language. It is precisely Wright's discomfort with both folk and modernist discourses that accounts for the blues power of his novel. The intensity of *Native Son*, its implicit call, derives from its indirect articulation of exclusion, of an experience which by its very nature cannot be rendered directly. Bigger Thomas's inability to sound a call *is* his call; his despair of envisioning a response *is* his response to the alienation of the Afro-American community in the modernist waste land.

Despite, or perhaps because of, Bigger's sense of exclusion from the Afro-American community, *Native Son* portrays him as a truly representative figure, a leader whose call attracts the validation of a strong communal response, though neither leader nor congregation is aware of the ritual Wright unconsciously articulates. Bigger repeatedly senses his connection with other blacks. In one sequence of fewer than ten pages, Wright establishes the underlying blues experience Bigger shares with the other black characters. Wright introduces the sequence with Bigger's meditation on this common experience, which includes the sense of alienation from the black community which keeps him from articulating his thoughts, in the form of a blues call: "Each person lived in one room and had a little world of his own. He hated this room and all the people in it, including himself. Why did he and his folks have to live like this? What had they ever done? Perhaps they had not done anything. Maybe they had to live this way precisely because none of them in all their lives had ever done anything, right or wrong, that mattered much" (p. 90 [100]). He sees his own sense

147

of exclusion reflected in his brother: "Looking at Buddy and thinking of Jan and Mr. Dalton, he saw in Buddy a certain stillness, an isolation, meaninglessness" (p. 92 [103]). Although he cannot openly acknowledge the blues link, Bigger knows that his friend Gus shares many of his feelings: "he knew Gus, as he knew himself, and he knew that one of them might fail through fear at the decisive moment" (p. 98 [110]). Despite his alienation from women, Bigger perceives the shared weariness of his mother and sister: "though [Vera's] face was smaller and smoother than his mother's, the beginning of the same tiredness was already there" (p. 92 [104]).

The association of the blues life with black women provides an important blues subtext of *Native Son*. A major theme in Baker's exploration of blues expression concerns the way in which economic oppression distorts relationships between black men and black women, both of whom are trapped in a discourse that all but precludes deep contact. As many feminist critics have demonstrated, a deep current of misogyny runs through Wright's work. Yet *Native Son* demonstrates at least a subliminal awareness of the nature of the problem. Bigger and Bessie's entire relationship is predicated on money: the money needed to buy the whiskey which Bigger in effect exchanges for sex. While Bigger does nothing to challenge or alter these relationships, Wright does not simply endorse the underlying sexist power structure. In a passage which culminates in Bigger's acknowledgment that Bessie likes him because "he gave her money for drinks," Wright intimates that such forces condition the life of the entire Afro-American community. Ironically, Bigger's refusal to respond to Bessie's suggestion that he articulate his experience sparks one of Wright's clearest articulations of the blues experience: "Her voice had come in a whisper, a whisper he had heard many times when she wanted something badly. It brought to him a full sense of her life, what he had been thinking and feeling when he had placed his hand upon her shoulder." Bigger explicitly associates his internal response to Bessie's whispered call with his earlier awareness of his family's suffering: "The same deep realization he had had that morning at home at the breakfast table while watching Vera and Buddy and his mother came back to him; only it was Bessie he was looking at now and seeing how blind she was. He felt the narrow orbit of her life" (p. 118 [131]). Which is, of course, the narrow orbit of his own. Shortly before her death, Bessie articulates her own sense of exclusion in a long blues moan beginning, "All my life's been full of hard trouble. If I wasn't hungry, I was sick. And if I wasn't sick, I was in trouble" (p. 194 [215]). Although he has previously arrived at similar perceptions, Bigger has no vocabulary capable of providing a response, of creating a space in which he and Bessie could acknowledge the depth of their shared blues life.

Despite his feeling of being "alone, profoundly, inescapably" (p. 264 [288]), Bigger repeatedly feels a desire for the affirmation encoded in the call-and-response dynamic. His thoughts in the prison cell reflect both his personal anguish and his creator's dissatisfaction with the solipsistic tendencies of modernist aesthetics: "why did not he hear resounding echoes of his feelings in the hearts of others? There were times when he did hear echoes, but always they were couched in tones which, living as a Negro, he could not answer or accept" (p. 264 [288]). As Bigger becomes more aware of his situation, his desire for a response to his call increases: "he wondered wistfully if there was not a set of words which he had in common with others, words which would evoke in others a sense of the same fire that smoldered in him" (pp. 308–9 [337]).

Bigger attempts to break through the encompassing silence three times in "Fate," once with his family and twice with Boris Max. When his family visits him in the prison cell, he responds to their suffering with the defiant compassion typical of the blues attitude: "he tried to think of words that would defy [the whites], words that would let them know that he had a world and life of his own in spite of them. And at the same time he wanted those words to stop the tears of his mother and sister, to quiet and soothe the anger of his brother" (p. 252 [275]). This desire translates into an awareness of his actual bonds with the Afro-American community: "No matter how much he would long for them to forget him, they would not be able to. His family was a part of him, not only in blood, but in spirit" (p. 254 [277]). Bigger's failure to articulate these feelings – to make the call – reflects Wright's limited apprehension of the Afro-American vernacular tradition. Immediately after the intensely significant embrace of the Thomas family, which takes place under the eyes of the whites in the cell, Bigger's mother begins to grovel before the Daltons, echoing the self-demeaning religious passivity Wright has previously attributed to Reverend Hammond. Wright's conscious sense of the limitations of black folk culture precludes the possibility of any positive image of call and response between Bigger and his family.

Bigger's two attempts to tell his story to Max (pp. 298–300 [326–8], 352–9 [385–92]) are not successful. Grounded in his despair over his feeling of exclusion from the black community, Bigger turns to a white audience just as Wright sought some response from his white contemporaries, whether modernist or Communist. Partially because Max fails to apprehend the complexity of Bigger's humanity and partially because of the inadequacy of the available discourses, both attempts collapse. In the final pages of *Native Son*, Bigger comes close to an adequate articulation of his experience. But the articulation receives no response. Max withdraws, abandoning Bigger to the modernist solipsism which has been the undercurrent of his experience throughout: "Bigger's voice died; he was listening to the echoes of his words in his own mind" (p. 335 [388]).

Reflecting the "near-tragic, near-comic lyricism" Ellison identified as the core of "Richard Wright's Blues," Bigger's response to his own call takes the form of the haunting laughter which echoes through the final pages of the novel. After Max's refusal to respond to the intensity of his call becomes clear, "Bigger laughed." When Max, typically unfamiliar with the Afro-American vernacular tradition, reacts with surprise, Bigger explains, "I ain't going to cry" (p. 358 [391]). The final image of Bigger reiterates the blues resonance of his situation: "Then he smiled a faint, wry, bitter smile. He heard the ring of steel against steel as a far door clanged shut" (p. 359 [392]). Bigger is most certainly, to use Langston Hughes's classic definition of the blues, "laughing to keep from crying." Yet the laughter – much bleaker than either Hughes's or Ellison's, sharing the solipsistic intensity of Samuel Beckett, the tormented isolation of Robert Johnson – is neither Bigger's nor Wright's alone. It echoes throughout *Native Son*. From the time Bigger leaves his family in their apartment until he reaches the Daltons, there are at least a dozen references to laughter. Bigger laughs. Gus laughs. Jack and G. H. laugh. Doc laughs. After the final outburst of blues laughter, Bigger says "I laughed so hard I cried" (p. 35 [43]). Incorporating Afro- and Euro-American sensibilities, establishing and repudiating bonds, feeling excluded from them all, *Native Son* resounds with a painful blues laughter, echoing through a modernist waste land which may or may not respond.

NOTES

1. Lillian S. Robinson and Lise Vogel, "Modernism and History," in *Sex, Class, & Culture,* by Lillian Robinson (New York: Methuen, 1978), p. 28.
2. Ibid., p.45.
3. Ibid., p.26.
4. Ralph Ellison, "Richard Wright's Blues," in his *Shadow and Act* (New York: New American Library, 1966), p. 100.
5. Ralph Ellison, "The World and the Jug," in his *Shadow and Act* (New York: New American Library, 1966), pp. 121–2.
6. Robert B. Stepto, "I thought I Knew These People: Richard Wright and the Afro-American Literary Tradition," in Michael S. Harper and Robert B.Stepto, eds., *Chant of Saints: A Gathering of Afro-American Literature, Art, and Scholarship* (Urbana: University of Illinois Press, 1979), p. 197.
7. Ibid., p. 198.
8. Ibid., p. 201.
9. Robert B. Stepto, *From Behind the Veil: A Study of Afro-American Narrative* (Urbana: University of Illinois Press, 1979), p. 167.
10. Stepto, "I Thought I Knew These People," p. 207.
11. W. E. B. Du Bois, *Writings* (New York: Library of America, 1986), p. 364.
12. See the introduction to this volume.
13. Richard Wright, *Native Son* (New York: Harper, 1940), p. 188 [208]. Subsequent parenthetical references are to this edition; for the reader's convenience bracketed page references to the Perennial Classic edition will also be provided.
14. Richard Wright, *How "Bigger" Was Born* (New York: Harper, 1940), p. 22.
15. [Richard Wright], "Portrait of Harlem," in *New York Panorama* (New York: Random House, 1938), p. 143.

16. Richard Wright, *American Hunger* (New York: Harper & Row, 1977), p. 22.
17. Wright, *How "Bigger" Was Born*, p. 28.
18. Richard Wright, "Introduction," in St. Clair Drake and Horace R. Cayton, *Black Metropolis: A Study of Negro Life in a Northern City* (New York: Harcourt Brace, 1945; rpt. New York: Harper & Row, 1962), p. xvii.
19. Monique Chefdor, "Modernism: Babel Revisited?" in Monique Chefdor, Ricardo Quinones, and Albert Wachtel, eds, *Modernism: Challenges and Perspectives* (Urbana: University of Illinois Press, 1986), p. 1.
20. Wright, *How "Bigger" Was Born*, pp. 7, 8, 19.
21. Ibid., p. 18.
22. Ellison, "The World and the Jug," p. 121.
23. Wright, *How "Bigger" Was Born*, p. 26.
24. Ibid., pp. 1–2, 2.
25. Ricardo Quinones, "From Resistance to Reassessment," in *Modernism: Challenges and Perspectives*, pp. 7–8.
26. Charles Baxter, "Assaulting the Audience in Modernism," in *Modernism: Challenges and Perspectives*, pp. 275, 276.
27. Bertolt Brecht, "Against Georg Lukács," in *Aesthetics and Politics* (London: Verso, 1980), p. 83.
28. Ibid., pp. 80–1.
29. Richard Wright, *Black Boy* (New York: Harper, 1945), p. 33.
30. Richard Wright, "Blueprint for Negro Writing," in Ellen Wright and Michel Fabre, eds., *Richard Wright Reader* (New York: Harper & Row, 1978), p. 41.
31. Wright, *How "Bigger" Was Born*, p. 25.
32. Richard Wright, "Foreword," in Paul Oliver, *Blues Fell This Morning* (London: Horizon Press, 1960), p. viii.
33. Richard Wright, *12 Million Black Voices: A Folk History of the Negro in the United States* (New York: Viking, 1941), p. 128.
34. Ron Karenga, "Black Cultural Nationalism," in Addison Gayle, Jr., ed., *The Black Aesthetic* (Garden City, N.Y.: Doubleday, 1972), p. 36.
35. Wright, "Foreword," p. ix.
36. Ibid., p. x.
37. Ellison, "Richard Wright's Blues," p. 90.
38. Houston A. Baker, Jr., *Blues, Ideology, and Afro-American Literature: A Vernacular Theory* (Chicago: University of Chicago Press, 1984), p. 147.

Notes on Contributors

Houston A. Baker, Jr., is Albert M. Greenfield Professor of Human Relations at the University of Pennsylvania. His books include *Singers of Daybreak: Studies in Black American Literature; The Journey Back: Issues in Black Literature and Criticism; Blues, Ideology, and Afro-American Literature: A Vernacular Theory; Modernism and the Harlem Renaissance;* and, most recently, *Afro-American Poetics.* He has edited numerous other volumes and also writes poetry, most recently collected in *Blues Journeys Home.*

Trudier Harris, J. Carlyle Sitterson Professor of English at the University of North Carolina at Chapel Hill, is the author of *From Mammies to Militants: Domestics in Black American Literature; Exorcising Blackness: Historical and Literary Lynching and Burning Rituals;* and *Black Women in the Fiction of James Baldwin,* as well as numerous essays on black literature and folklore. She has coedited three volumes and edited three additional volumes on Afro-American writers for the *Dictionary of Literary Biography* series.

Keneth Kinnamon is Ethel Pumphrey Stephens Professor of English and Chairman of the Department at the University of Arkansas. He has written *The Emergence of Richard Wright: A Study in Literature and Society* and, with the help of Joseph Benson, Michel Fabre, and Craig Werner, *A Richard Wright Bibliography.* He is the author of a monograph on James Baldwin and the editor of *James Baldwin: A Collection of Critical Essays,* and with Richard K. Barksdale the co-editor of *Black Writers of America.*

John M. Reilly serves as President of United University Professions of the State University of New York system and Vice-President of the American Federation of Teachers, AFL-CIO, as well as Professor of English at the State University of New York, Albany. A veteran Wright scholar, he has edited *Richard Wright: The Critical Reception* and written many articles on the author. He also writes extensively on popular literature and won the Edgar Allan Poe Award of the Mystery Writers of America in 1981.

Craig Werner, Professor of Afro-American Studies at the University of Wisconsin–Madison, works on Anglo-American modernism and postmodernism as well as, and in relation to, Afro-American literature. His books are *Paradoxical Resolutions: American Fiction Since James Joyce; Dubliners: A Pluralistic World;* and *Adrienne Rich: The Poet and Her Critics.* His essays have treated Baldwin, Baraka, Ellison, Faulkner, Knight, Morrison, Reed, and numerous others.

Selected Bibliography

Citations of *Native Son* in this volume are to the first edition (New York: Harper, 1940); for the reader's convenience bracketed references to the more widely available Perennial Classic paperback edition are also provided.

The basic bibliographical tools for a study of Richard Wright are Charles T. Davis and Michel Fabre, *Richard Wright: A Primary Bibliography* (Boston: G. K. Hall, 1982), which lists unpublished as well as published works, and *A Richard Wright Bibliography: Fifty Years of Criticism and Commentary, 1933–1982* (Westport, Conn.: Greenwood Press, 1988), compiled by Keneth Kinnamon with the help of Joseph Benson, Michel Fabre, and Craig Werner. The latter volume is comprehensive, containing 13,117 annotated items. Michel Fabre has written a notable biography, *The Unfinished Quest of Richard Wright* (New York: William Morrow, 1973). The following list of books provides various perspectives on Wright and *Native Son*.

Abcarian, Richard, ed. *Richard Wright's Native Son: A Critical Handbook.* Belmont, Cal.: Wadsworth, 1970.

Baker, Houston A., Jr., ed. *Twentieth Century Interpretations of Native Son: A Collection of Critical Essays.* Englewood Cliffs, N.J.: Prentice-Hall, 1972.

Bakish, David. *Richard Wright.* New York: Ungar, 1973.

Baldwin, James. *Notes of a Native Son.* Boston: Beacon Press, 1955.

Bell, Bernard W. *The Afro-American Novel and Its Tradition.* Amherst: University of Massachusetts Press, 1987.

Bigsby, C. W. E. *The Second Black Renaissance: Essays in Black Literature.* Westport, Conn.: Greenwood Press, 1980.

Bone, Robert A. *The Negro Novel in America.* Revised edition. New Haven, Conn.: Yale University Press, 1965.

Brignano, Russell Carl. *Richard Wright: An Introduction to the Man and His Works.* Pittsburgh: University of Pittsburgh Press, 1970.

Burgum, Edwin Berry. *The Novel and the World's Dilemma.* New York: Oxford University Press, 1947.

Cooke, Michael G. *Afro-American Literature in the Twentieth Century: The Achievement of Intimacy.* New Haven, Conn.: Yale University Press, 1984.

Ellison, Ralph. *Shadow and Act.* New York: Random House, 1964.

Fabre, Michel. *The World of Richard Wright.* Jackson: University Press of Mississippi, 1985.

Felgar, Robert. *Richard Wright.* Boston: Twayne, 1980.

Fishburn, Katherine. *Richard Wright's Hero: The Faces of a Rebel-Victim.* Metuchen, N.J.: Scarecrow Press, 1977.

Gayle, Addison, Jr. *The Way of the New World: The Black Novel in America.* Garden City, N.Y.: Anchor Press/Doubleday, 1975.

Gibson, Donald B. *The Politics of Literary Expression: A Study of Major Black Writers.* Westport, Conn.: Greenwood Press, 1981.

Gysin, Fritz. *The Grotesque in American Negro Fiction: Jean Toomer, Richard Wright, and Ralph Ellison.* Bern: Francke Verlag, 1975.

Hakutani, Yoshinobu, ed. *Critical Essays on Richard Wright.* Boston: G. K. Hall, 1982.

Joyce, Joyce A. *Richard Wright's Art of Tragedy.* Iowa City: University of Iowa Press, 1986.

Kinnamon, Keneth. *The Emergence of Richard Wright: A Study in Literature and Society.* Urbana: University of Illinois Press, 1972.

Macksey, Richard, and Moorer, Frank E., eds. *Richard Wright: A Collection of Critical Essays.* Englewood Cliffs, N.J.: Prentice-Hall, 1984.

Margolies, Edward. *The Art of Richard Wright.* Carbondale: Southern Illinois University Press, 1969.

McCall, Dan. *The Example of Richard Wright.* New York: Harcourt, Brace & World, 1969.

Payne, Ladell. *Black Novelists and the Southern Literary Tradition.* Athens: The University of Georgia Press, 1982.

Reilly, John M., ed. *Richard Wright: The Critical Reception.* New York: Burt Franklin, 1978.

Rosenblatt, Robert. *Black Fiction.* Cambridge, Mass.: Harvard University Press, 1974.

Schraufnagel, Noel. *From Apology to Protest: The Black American Novel.* DeLand, Florida: Everett/Edwards, 1973.

Smith, Valerie. *Self-Discovery and Authority in Afro-American Narrative.* Cambridge, Mass.: Harvard University Press, 1987.

Walker, Margaret. *Richard Wright; Daemonic Genius.* New York: Warner Books, 1988.

Webb, Constance. *Richard Wright: A Biography.* New York: Putnam's, 1968.